Seventeenth-Century England

Modern Scholarship on European History

Henry A. Turner, Jr.
General Editor

SOCIETY IN AN AGE OF REVOLUTION
EDITED WITH AN INTRODUCTION
BY PAUL S. SEAVER

New Viewpoints
A Division of Franklin Watts, New York, London, 1976

New Viewpoints
A Division of Franklin Watts
730 Fifth Avenue
New York, N.Y. 10019

Seventeenth-Century England

Library of Congress Cataloging in Publication Data
Main entry under title:

Seventeenth-century England.

  (Modern scholarship on European history).
  Includes bibliographical references and index.
  CONTENTS: Stone, L. Social mobility in England, 1500–1700.
—Thirsk, J. Seventeenth-century agriculture and social change.
[etc.]
    1. Great Britain—Economic conditions—Addresses, essays,
lectures. 2. England—Social conditions—Addresses, essays, lectures. 3. England—Politics and government—Addresses, essays,
lectures. I. Seaver, Paul S.
HC254.4.S48   309.1′42′05   75-11984

ISBN 0-531-05377-6
ISBN 0-531-05584-1 pbk.

Manufactured in the United States of America

6 5 4 3 2 1

Contents

Introduction

To present a collection of essays on seventeenth-century England that in no way directly deals with the mid-century civil wars and revolution may seem at the very least quixotic, if not misguided and perverse. Such an approach to what Christopher Hill has called "the Century of Revolution" may perhaps be excused on practical grounds, for collections and anthologies focusing on the mid-century crisis abound,[1] and the end of this spate of publication is not yet in sight.[2] Yet for all the attention historians have lavished on seventeenth-century England, there is no sign either that exhaustion has set in or that agreement has been reached on the nature of the crisis or on its larger significance.

For the big picture—the scope and significance of the changes brought about by the English revolution—remains a subject of continued controversy. Some Marxist historians are still prepared to maintain with various modifications that Clarendon's "Great Rebellion" was in essence the first bourgeois revolution or at least the first revolution of modernization.[3] Coming from the other end of the political spectrum, H. R. Trevor-Roper sees the Civil War as a "revolution of despair," launched by the backwoods gentry in a last, futile attempt to crush the bloated Renaissance monarchy whose values they did not share and whose policies they could not control.[4] Calling down a plague on both houses in the course of a brilliant critique of the "gentry controversy," the American liberal historian J. H. Hexter still finds most compelling a version of the older Whig view which sees the revolution as an acute constitutional crisis brought about by the inept authoritarianism of the Stuart monarchy.[5]

Historians have displayed the same lack of agreement on the larger significance or long-term consequences of the mid-century crisis. On the one hand, Christopher Hill sees vast consequences arising from the revolutionary decades, for although the traditional monarchy, church, and aristocracy returned at the Restoration, attempts to restrict and harness economic appetites for the common weal were at an end. Exploitation of the countryside by the dominant landed class was finally freed from Whitehall interference, foreign policy increasingly took cognizance of the needs of foreign trade, and the way was open for the commercial and agricultural revolutions that preceded the triumph of the bourgeoisie in the industrial revolution.[6] On the other hand, Lawrence Stone, while in no way denying that a true revolution took place, nevertheless sees its immediate consequences as slight in an era which saw the traditional court and peerage not only return but to some degree impose an even firmer grip on the country: "What was significant about the English Revolution was not its success in permanently changing the face of England—for this was slight—but the intellectual content of the various opposition programmes and achievements after 1640. . . . It is this legacy of ideas which makes it reasonable to claim that the crisis in England in the seventeenth century is the first 'Great Revolution' in the history of the world. . . ."[7] Finally, it has been argued that there is little point in searching for significance when little of consequence changed. The seventeenth century, G. R. Elton has complained, "remains, too readily, the 'century of revolution', even though it is becoming more and more apparent, all the noise of battle notwithstanding, that few things really changed, and that continuity is at least as notable as revolution."[8]

In part, the failure of most historians to accept Elton's dismissal is doubtless due, as Peter Laslett has remarked, to the natural disposition to feel that "great events have great causes. Anything as conspicuous, as interesting, and as influential as the only civil war in [English] history . . . must surely . . . have been a cataclysm, the climax of a process going deep down into the social fabric and extending over many generations, backwards and forwards in time."[9] In part, such profound disagreement is doubtless due to what C. H. George has called the polemical and philosophical inclinations of the historians involved. Certainly ideological differences are present and in some instances probably determinant.[10]

At times even agreement is more apparent than real. G. R. Elton and Peter Laslett both deny that significant change took place in seventeenth-century England, but the apparent agreement is fortuitous. For Elton a true revolution had taken place in the 1530s under the aegis of Thomas Cromwell, the impact of whose reforms were more truly revolutionary and long-lasting than the more dramatic events associated with Oliver Cromwell a century later. On the other hand, Laslett, who is concerned less with government than with society, with what he calls "the passing of the traditional world," denies that this traumatic passing can be dated before the arrival of the factory system in the mid- and late eighteenth century. Only then does he find "those changes of scale, that sense of alienation of the worker from his work, that breach of continuity of emotional experience," that alone marks the coming of modern industrial society.[11]

Sometimes apparent agreement disguises not so much a difference in what is regarded as significant in history as a difference in perspective which grants to one observer a breadth of judgement, a longer view, denied to another. Both Sir John Oglander, a seventeenth-century Hampshire gentleman, and G. E. Aylmer, presently professor of history at the University of York, discern changes in the 1640s and 1650s of a magnitude that can only be seen as a major social cataclysm. However, while Sir John chronicled what he clearly regarded as the unprecedented slaughter of his order—"there were in Yorkshire a hundred families extinct or undone, so that none of them could appear again as gentlemen. Death, plunder, sales and sequestrations sent them to another world or beggars' bush, and so all—or most—shires"—Aylmer, with the added perspective of time and systematic study, admits that while the "Civil War and the republic undoubtedly saw a shift within the landowning class," this revolution was, nevertheless, "partial, uncompleted, and ultimately unsuccessful."[12]

The attempt to sort out these distinctions and differences is obviously useful, for until we do so we will continue to talk past each other, neither confronting our opponents squarely nor meeting a real confrontation in return, all of which may produce a noisy battle but nevertheless one without decisive results. Certainly the continuation of the larger debate is inevitable, given the very real stakes involved in our understanding of the nature and dynamics of historical change. However, my purpose here is more modest. While the articles assembled in this collection do not deal directly with the mid-century revolution, they do examine both some of the basic structures that defined the English society which underwent revolution and some of the basic social and political attitudes that shaped and set limits to the extent of change. Several years ago Lawrence Stone observed that, while the gentry controversy of the 1950s had reduced agreement on almost every important aspect of the problem virtually "to zero," the last twenty years have neverthe-less seen "the most remarkable efflorescence of specialized histori-cal monographs, the work of scholars on both sides of the Atlantic who have been prepared to take infinite pains . . . and who have also had the insight, imagination, and intellectual capacity to marshal their findings and to generalize from them." The special-ized works have been accompanied by an equally remarkable proliferation of studies which attempt to erect larger structures on the basis of the new research, larger pictures of how aspects or sectors of English society worked, and which must be seen funda-mentally as invitations by their authors to their colleagues to try on the new generalizations. The essays brought together here are drawn both from the specialized studies and from the more general and theoretical work published in the past twenty years. It is hoped that the reader will find in them, as Lawrence Stone concluded, that "a good deal of light is at last beginning to penetrate the fog."[13]

To insist that no significant change took place in seventeenth-century England, or that the only significant change occurred in the course of the mid-century cataclysm, seems to imply either an unnecessarily olympian view or an unfortunate myopia. The im-portance of the revolution of the 1640s and 1650s is in no way diminished by suggesting that other, if more gradual, changes were in the making during the course of the century. Further, the long view that measures significant change only in terms of the transfor-mation of traditional society into its modern industrial successor may lead one to overlook the perhaps more subtle but no less profound changes that would permit one to define English society, like that of the Dutch, as essentially "modern" by 1700, although not yet industrialized. Such a thesis is at least arguable, and has been so argued recently by E. A. Wrigley.[14] Be that as it may, and ignoring for the moment the vexed question of significance, England in 1700 presents to even the superficial observer a very different image from that of England in the last years of Queen Elizabeth's reign. England in the early seventeenth century was blessed with a monarch as fundamentally pacific as his predecessor. Having terminated hostilities by proclamation, King James in 1604 brought an end to the war with Spain which England could neither win nor her Parliaments adequately pay for. By the end of the century James's great-grandson, William III, led a European coalition against the Sun King himself in a series of military confrontations which the nation could now manage, if not perhaps easily afford, by means of a national debt funded by the new Bank of England, and backed by the taxing powers of Parliament itself. In the first decade of the eighteenth century English-led armies were to return triumphantly to the Continent, and, as in the days of Crecy and Agincourt, England was once more one of the two major European powers.

If one turns from international standing to domestic culture, the appearance of change is equally obvious. The early years of the century marked the heyday of the English Renaissance; in the last years England entered the Augustan world. The late Elizabethan aristocrats had themselves painted as icons, as formal representations of virtuous peers and magistrates;[15] the Caroline Court aristocracy, following the royal example, saw themselves in Van Dyke's portraits in all their worried individuality, introspective and melancholic, as well they might be, given the progressive isolation of the Court from the country in the 1630s. By contrast in the 1660s the Earl of Sunderland had himself painted confidently clothed in a Roman toga amidst classical surroundings, and by the end of the century Godfrey Kneller portrayed an English peerage not only evidently proud but even a shade complacent.[16] Stylistic change was not, of course, confined to portraiture. The transformation of prose style, nowhere more evident than in the approved rhetoric in which sermons were preached, was equally marked.

During the first quarter of the century, the Court favoured and patronized the witty and metaphysical style of Bishop Lancelot Andrewes and Dean John Donne. In the latter half of the century popular preachers at Court, such as Archbishop Tillotson, used the plain style, a rhetoric hitherto championed by the popular Puritan sermonizers but now endorsed by the propagandist of the Royal Society itself as "a close, naked, natural way of speaking . . . bringing all things as near the Mathematical plainness as they can. . . ."[17]

The abandonment of one rhetorical style for another was but part of a more profound cultural change, a transformation that T. S. Eliot, who regretted it, termed the "dissociation of sensibility" and which saw the erosion of the traditional world view. The universe, which was understood to be composed of species and elements qualitatively distinguishable according to their essences and attributes, arranged hierarchically as they were created by God from greatest to least, from superior to inferior, and, hence, capable of being argued about by analogy—this traditional universe gradually gave way to one distinguishable by quantities rather than qualities, and, hence, to one subjected to mathematical analysis. Alongside arguments using analogy and similitude, so beloved by King James—"Kings are justly called Gods, for that they exercise a manner or resemblance of Divine power upon earth"[18]— the political arithmeticians of the second half of the century employed their new quantitative analysis. "For (instead of using only comparative and superlative words, and intellectual arguments)," Sir William Petty explained in 1677, "I have taken the course (as a specimen of the Political Arithmetic I have long aimed at) to express myself in Terms of Number, Weight or Measure. . . ."[19] Doubtless much was lost in the course of such a profound cultural change. As John Donne anticipated as early as 1612 in his *First Anniversarie,* not only did the "New Philosophy" call all in doubt, but it also made poetry as he knew it impossible.

> What Artist now dares boast that he can bring
> Heaven hither, or constellate any thing,
> So as the influence of those stars may bee
> Imprison'd in an Hearbe, or Charme, or Tree,
> And doe by touch, all which those stars could doe?
> The art is lost, and correspondence too.

If the correspondence between different realms of being drawn by analogy and similitude lost its reality, the metaphysical conceit became not so much a sudden illuminating truth as a mere rhetorical trick. Nevertheless, if the new philosophy of number, weight, and measure destroyed one world, it opened the way for another, simpler, if less human, universe—that of Sir Isaac Newton.

Like the changes in its international standing and in its internal culture, the transformation of English society was no less real for all that it was gradual and incomplete. Part of our difficulty in understanding the nature and extent of this transformation is due to the vast differences in scale and the difficulty in drawing comparisons that illuminate rather than distort. England and Wales in 1600 had a population less than a tenth that of the present-day United Kingdom. With a population of approximately 4,500,000 there were about the same number of subjects of James I as there are present-day citizens of Finland. England in the seventeenth century was primarily a rural society; as late as 1690 estimates based on Gregory King's figures suggest that only 15 percent of the population lived in towns of 1,000 or larger, whereas in 1968, 49 percent of the population of the United Kingdom lived in urban centers of 100,000 or larger. Most Englishmen were still primarily engaged in agricultural production: for example, almost 70 percent of the inhabitants of Worcestershire in the first half of the seventeenth century were so engaged, and in all probability much of the remaining 30 percent were dependent on agricultural production in one way or another (agriculture plus the textile, clothing, and leather industries accounted for about 80 percent of the work force; the same four occupations accounted for about 78 percent of the work force of Elizabethan Oxfordshire and about 82 percent of the work force of rural mid-Essex in the later seventeenth and early eighteenth century). The population of seventeenth-century England was also a younger one than that found today in the British Isles: at the end of the seventeenth century about 28 percent of the population was under the age of ten, whereas in 1961 only about 15 percent fell within that age range; in fact, the age distribution in seventeenth-century England more closely resembles that of present-day India (about 30 percent under the age of ten in 1961) or Ceylon (about 29 percent in 1955) than Western Europe in recent times. Further, the productive lives of seventeenth-century Englishmen were shorter, only about 24 percent of the population being in the forty or older age group, whereas in 1958 some 44 percent of the population of England and Wales fell into that category. Given such a population profile, it is perhaps no wonder that Defoe, that champion of trade and manufacturing, should have seen child labor as so beneficent. Noting the many advantages of the Yorkshire dales, he remarked that "no hands being unemployed, all can gain their bread, even from the youngest to the ancient; hardly anything above four years old, but its hands are sufficient unto itself."[20]

It is tempting to see such a largely rural, agrarian country with its young population and its high death rate as analogous to the modern so-called under-developed countries, and in a number of obvious ways such a comparison is legitimate and revealing. Nevertheless, by viewing England in this way, two important aspects are apt to be overlooked. First, while seventeenth-century England was obviously underdeveloped in the sense of being pre-industrial, its economy and society were not notably backward by comparison with other Western European nations. No longer was it, as it had been centuries earlier, an essentially colonial economy, exporting raw materials—wool and tin—to the more advanced continental manufacturing and marketing areas. Nor was England technologically backward: the stocking frame had been invented by a Nottinghamshire parson toward the end of Elizabeth's reign; the slitting mill was introduced in the iron industry in the early seventeenth century; in 1698 Savery patented his steam engine; and by the end of the first decade of the eighteenth century Abraham Darby had begun to use coke in his blast furnaces.[21] England was pre-industrial but not economically or technologically backward by the standards of the age.

Secondly, to focus on the pre-industrial aspects of the society disguises the degree to which a traditional society was being transformed from within by a variety of changes. First of all, the total population, which numbered about 4.5 millions in 1600 had grown from perhaps a mere 3 millions in 1500 and was to continue to grow to about 5.5 millions by 1700, but that growth was to be far from even. Life expectancy at birth, which had averaged about forty-three years between 1538 and 1624 in Colyton, Devonshire, fell to thirty-seven years for the last three quarters of the seventeenth century.[22] In the middle years of Elizabeth's reign Hakluyt noted that "throughe oure longe peace and seldome sickness we are growen more populous than ever heretofore,"[23] but in the 1620s sickness returned with a vengeance, led by a catastrophic visitation of the plague in 1625, which continued to return till its last violent outbreak in 1665 and which was accompanied by smallpox, influenza, and typhus, which collectively were scarcely less serious scourges. In some parishes by about 1640 more deaths than births were recorded, a condition which recurred in bad years well into the 1680s.[24] Further, the effects of disease were compounded by changing patterns of marriage and childbearing. Whereas E. A. Wrigley found that in the forty years after 1560 Colyton women averaged twenty-seven years of age at the time they first married, the average age of first marriage rose with obvious consequences for fertility to thirty years in the 1647-59 period and did not again drop as low as twenty-seven until the second quarter of the eighteenth century.[25] Late marriage provides one means of population limitation, spacing children another, and Colyton families which on the average had delayed about three years (37.5 months) between the next to the last and the last child in the family in the years 1560–1646, then waited even longer between the penultimate and final conception (50.7 months average) in the years between 1647 and 1719. An obvious consequence of such measures was the drop in the number, never great at best, of large families in Colyton, for whereas 55 percent of the women who married under thirty and lived through their fertile period had six or more children in the two generations after 1560, only 18 percent had six or more in the years between 1646 and 1719.[26]

Obviously, population growth on this scale, particularly far from uniform growth, did not take place without affecting society as a whole. The price index for a fixed market basket of consumables, reflecting the consumption patterns of a laborer, which had hovered around 100 in the years from 1490 to 1512, thereafter began to rise, reaching an average of 500 between 1596 and 1605. Although there were other factors which contributed to the price rise, the fact that real wages, expressed in terms of the same unit of consumables, fell by about 50 percent by 1590 suggests that the increase in the population from 3 to 4.5 millions pressed heavily on food supplies and on other basic consumption items while the growing labor force depressed real wages. The price index rose into the 600s during the 1630s, but thereafter, despite fluctuations, did not again begin a consistent upward course until the 1760s. Again, the correlation with the demographic trend is noticeable, and the consequences unsurprising—wages which had not risen appreciably since the 1570s again began a slow upward climb after 1630.[27]

If the price rise had worked a hardship on some, it had obviously benefited others, and the buoyant agricultural prices must have been to the advantage of both the direct producer and the landowner who succeeded in raising rents at a rate commensurate with the rise in agricultural prices.[28] The rise in the standard of living was conspicuous among the yeomen and gentry; the Elizabethan parson William Harrison noted how pewter had replaced wooden tableware, how glass windows had become commonplace, all within his lifetime, and the modern historian W. B. Hoskins sees what he has called "the rebuilding of rural England" as taking place in the years between 1570 and 1640.[29] At the same time the incentive for increasing agricultural production was continuous, and Eric Kerridge posits an agricultural revolution as taking place in the century after 1560, although not completed until the early eighteenth century.[30] Technical innovation and regional specialization led to growing production, and, as Joan Thirsk shows in her essay reprinted here, fears that the overproduction of grain would drive down prices were already current even before the population ceased its rapid expansion in the decades after 1630. After the Restoration grain prices fell despite occasional exports. Wool prices, which had never risen as fast as food prices in the sixteenth century, ceased to rise substantially after the first decade of the seventeenth century, and, like grain prices, the Restoration saw a long decline also in the price of this commodity.

If the domestic economy presented at best a bracing climate and an increasingly competitive market as population growth slowed, the overseas sector presented a more expansive picture as the century progressed. Although in terms of gross national product, foreign trade even at the end of the century constituted no more than 10 percent of the total, Ralph Davis has recently suggested that in the late seventeenth century "more than a quarter of all manufacturing production, a half of the production of woollen goods, was exported" and "nearly a quarter of home consumption of manufactures was imported. . . ."[31] Further, not only did trade expand in value some 500 percent in the course of the seventeenth century, but the trading area of English shippers expanded radically as well with all that such expansion implied for capital investment and the increased employment of seamen and others in ancillary occupations. Trade, which in Tudor times had been dominated by the short haul across the Channel to Antwerp and later across the North Sea to Amsterdam, Hamburg, and Emden, came in the Stuart century to stretch from Danzig at the northern end to Constantinople at the southern end of the European axis of English trade, and from Barbados in the west to India in the east. Further, at the same time that extra-European trade employed increasing quantities of shipping, local coasting shipping grew, spurred on by such increasingly important commodities as sea coal, the Tyneside shipment of which multiplied some ten times in the course of the seventeenth century. Sixteenth-century trade had been dominated by cloth exports, and up to the civil wars cloth remained the dominant export, although the more heterogeneous, specialized, and lighter textiles of the New Draperies gradually supplanted such older exports as the traditional Western broadcloths and Northern kerseys destined for northern and eastern European markets. By 1700 woollen textiles made up less than half (48 percent) of the total exports, and the role the new, lighter cloths of the New Draperies had come to play can be seen in the fact that, by 1700, 40 percent of all textile exports were destined for the Mediterranean, and these constituted 70 percent of all exports to southern Europe and Turkey. There is no reason to suppose that textile exports declined absolutely. What accounts for the relative displacement was the rapid expansion of the re-export trade in such colonial and Asian products as tobacco, sugar, and calico. In 1621, 94 percent of all imports had come from Europe; by 1700 about 35 percent came from the Americas and Asia and almost 40 percent of the trade to northern Europe was made up of the re-export of these exotic products.[32]

This mixed picture of a population which grew rapidly until the

1630s, of rents and agricultural prices which remained buoyant until the mid-century, and of an overseas trade which expanded very rapidly in the latter half of the century, provides a background for Lawrence Stone's pioneering study of social mobility, reprinted here. Something like a century of relatively high mobility came to an end in the middle of the seventeenth century, but the increasing stability and rigidity of Restoration society nevertheless left England in 1700 with a rather different social profile, one in which the tiny traditional social élite of wealthy landowners— gentlemen and peers—had been joined by "a series of more or less independent economic and status hierarchies" of which "church, law, commerce, and government office are the most conspicuous." This state of affairs was not necessarily one welcomed by the traditional élite. As early as the 1670s an observer noted that the gentry used education as one means of segregating the social orders: "The gentry . . . without censure keep their blood unmixt with mean conversation, by immurring them at home, or sequestring them into some convenient recess, to be trained up in society with their equals."[33] By Queen Anne's reign the complaints levelled against the "moneyed interest" were common—bitter testimony to the reality of social change.[34]

One important aspect of seventeenth-century English society is apt to be overlooked by a too exclusive concentration on the big picture, and that is the pervasive nature of provincial diversity. As Alan Everitt has pointed out, even the national élite of the Parliamentary gentry continued to marry in their neighborhoods, and, as late as the Long Parliament in the 1640s only some twenty Yorkshire families had London town houses.[35] The national patterns of mobility that Stone analyzes were cut across by provincial deviations from the norm. Thus, while there is no reason to doubt Stone's estimate that the number of armigerous gentry families trebled in the period, the distribution of recently risen families and the degree to which such families were new to the shire community varied widely. In Kent, a stronghold of conservative insularity, 90 percent of the gentry of 1640 either stemmed from medieval Kentish freeholders or Tudor yeomen of the shire; in Northamptonshire, on the other hand, only 50 percent of the shire élite were of ancient native stock.[36] The significance of the increase in the numbers of the landed élite can be viewed in another way: in Buckinghamshire and Rutland in 1522, as Stone notes, only one village in ten had a resident squire; by 1680, nationally, two out of every three villages seems to have been presided over by one or more members of the gentry.[37] Yet, as Everitt points out, such statistical generalizations disguise substantial regional diversity. Whereas in the champion country of open fields and of sheep and corn production village after village was dominated by the manor houses of the resident gentry, in such pastoral areas as the Weald of Kent, Everitt found a weak manorial structure, a large number of yeoman farmers but few resident gentry, a variety of agricultural pursuits but also an increasing industrial by-employment which supplemented the farming incomes of the growing population.[38]

Joan Thirsk's essay on "Seventeenth-Century Agriculture and Social Change" explores this regional diversity and the increasingly socially diverse communities which changing economic opportunity produced. For what becomes evident the moment one looks beyond the great uniformities of the social hierarchy is the almost infinite variety of the peasant communities hidden beneath the common terms of so many yeomen, so many husbandmen and laborers. Not only was the peasantry on the whole better off in the pastoral and forest parishes than in the fielden, but the tendency was for the population to grow more rapidly in these favored communities than in the open-field, grain-growing areas. Further, specialization and industrialization both developed most markedly in these areas and in the occasional fielden parish which duplicated their weak manorialism and populousness. In Wigston Magna in Leicestershire the demesne lands had been sold to the wealthier tenants at the turn of the century; the population grew at the same time that land was consolidated into larger farms; and by the second half of the seventeenth century much of the surplus labor found employment in framework-knitting.[39] For all that many elements of diversity were old, based as they were on traditionally different communities, much of the seventeenth-century development, in particular the regional specialization and increasing industrialization, is best seen as a rationalization of the rural economy —in short, of its modernization.

Acting like a forced draft on the regional economies, increasing both the degree of specialization and industrialization, was London, James I's "great wen." A frightening problem for the monarchy as well as for its own magistracy, London was, nevertheless, perhaps the single most important factor in the modernization of seventeenth-century England. London doubled in size in the seventeenth century, while the total population of England grew only about 22 percent. In the course of this phenomenal growth London became the largest city in Europe, but more significantly for seventeenth-century England it dwarfed all other urban centers. At the beginning of the century London had been perhaps five times the size of Norwich, the largest provincial town; by the end of the century London was fifteen times as large.[40] In the early Elizabethan period London was already recognized as the center of fashion; as John Hall wrote in 1565: "For they of the country ever take heed/How they of the City do wear their weed."[41] In the seventeenth century, as F. J. Fisher has recently noted, England's trade shifted from being export-led to import-led, a shift which in the latter part of the century on the external side was largely paid for by re-exports. The center of this consumption-led trade was London itself, generating a market-garden development in the Thames Valley and elsewhere in proximity to the city, buying its fuel from Newcastle, encouraging by its existence not only regional specialization but also national integration, such as, for example, its cutlery industry, which used Sheffield blades, and its clock industry, which depended on parts made in far-off Lancashire.[42] In fact, the shift of the iron industry from the vicinity of London to the north and west seems to have been due as much to the high food and labor costs in the neighborhood of London as to the exhaustion of local fuel. As a consequence, the Weald, where fifty-one of the fifty-eight (88 percent) blast furnaces in England had been located in 1553 lost steadily to the north and west, despite the expansion of the industry as a whole, and by 1653 the Weald was the source of less than 50 percent of the furnaces.[43] In effect, London provided the rapidly expanding market otherwise lacking following the demographic slow-down after 1630, but by the same token new industry seeking cheap labor was forced out of London's immediate neighborhood. The growing framework-knitting industry, though financed from London, developed in such villages as

Wigston Magna and around Nottingham and the villages surrounding Sherwood Forest.[44]

If London was the great engine, pushing England toward modernization and industrialization, it is nevertheless true that England's industrial "take-off" had not occurred by 1700. The need for steadily expanding demand seems to have been a crucial factor. The late J. D. Chambers argued in his recent, posthumously published book, that had the population growth, which seems to have begun in the 1690s, continued past the 1720s, the economic growth symbolized by the rapid expansion of the number of patents for invention and of building in London and elsewhere, by the first turnpikes and the first coking process, might have pushed forward the industrial revolution by a half-century or more.[45] Equally as crucial as sheer numbers was the creation of effective demand, and it is to this failure to produce an expanding mass market that D. C. Coleman's essay on labor in the seventeenth-century economy, reprinted here, addresses itself. As William Petty remarked in the 1670s, "It is observed by Clothiers and others, who employ great numbers of poor people, that when corn is extremely plentiful, that the labour of the poor is proportionately dear; and scarce to be had at all (so licentious are they who labour only to eat, or perhaps to drink)."[46]

The propensity of the laboring poor to prefer leisure to higher earnings was generally recognized and of long standing. In part it was due to the very nature of much pre-industrial labor, even in manufacturing. Until the advent of power-driven machinery, there was no need to work continuously at boring tasks, and until the development of highly integrated industries, interruptions were a regular part of the work pattern: weaving would stop while finished cloths were stretched on tenter hooks, and so on. In fact, E. P. Thompson had argued that a work pattern in which bouts of intense labor alternate with idleness appears "whenever men were in control of their own working lives" and may in fact be the "natural" human work rhythm.[47] Such traditional patterns can be and have been changed, but as later experience was to show, the necessary carrot and stick were absent in the pre-industrial world. For most seventeenth-century laborers there was neither evidence that long hours would appreciably raise his standard of living nor that the market would absorb ever-expanding quantities of goods. Given such an economic framework, the combination of industrial with other employment was almost inevitable: thus, Cornish tinners also fished, hand-loom weavers traditionally helped with the harvest, and much of the metal trades and mining was combined with smallholding.[48] Presumably the economically successful would have seen the force of Richard Baxter's stricture, when that Puritan moralist reminded his readers of the commonplace—"Remember how gainful the Redeeming of Time is . . . in Merchandize, or any trading; in husbandry or any gaining course. . . ."[49] For many workers whose club was the local tippling house, the following verse printed in 1639 may have come closer to expressing the ideal:

> You know that Munday is Sundayes brother;
> Tuesday is such another
> Wednesday you must go to Church and pray;
> Thursday is half-holiday;
> On Friday it is too late to begin to spin;
> The Saturday is half-holiday agen.[50]

If society, though changed and changing, remained unrevolutionized, surely social and political theory did not. At the beginning of the century King James's divine-right theory seemed orthodox and irrefutable at least in its premises; and such a theory of authority was entirely compatible with an organic view of society in which inequality was considered both natural and good. These traditional ideas were in fact commonplaces centuries old in the West.[51] The order presupposed was natural and good because given by God, but equally so because to the ultimate welfare of all members of the commonwealth: "So hath that great author of order distributed the ranks and offices of men in order to mutual benefit and comfort, that one man should plow, another thresh . . . another sail, another trade, another supervise all these, labouring to keep them all in order and peace; that one should work with his hands . . . another with his head . . . all conspiring to one common end, the welfare of the whole. . . ."[52] The only surprise in such sentiments is their publication in 1700, for they certainly express beliefs held unexceptional a century earlier. One assumes that somehow the mid-century convulsions had dissolved that older world view, that such theories had been ground small between the upper and nether millstones of Leveller democracy, which insisted on the existence of natural rights when historical precedent failed, and of Hobbes's atomistic men, who sought by a contract to erect Leviathan against presumably worse evils in a hostile social world. Surely Locke is the proper successor to the revolutionary decades, not Isaac Barrow, whose traditional views were quoted above.

Yet nothing is so evident as the persistence of traditional ideas about society and hence about authority and politics from one end of the century to the other. Traditional political relations had received a severe shake-up in the course of the revolution, but society came through relatively unscathed. Richard Baxter recognized as much in his assurance to parents in the 1670s that their traditional powers remained legitimate and unquestioned: "Your authority over children is most unquestionable. They will dispute the authority of ministers, yea, and of magistrates. . . . But the parents authority is beyond all dispute. . . . Therefore father and mother is the first natural power mentioned rather than kings or queens in the fifth commandment."[53] Patriarchalism may have survived largely unquestioned and intact, but recognition of its continued legitimacy does not imply necessarily that it was loved, as Aubrey's acid remark on the well-known hatred of children for their parents amply testifies: "The child perfectly loathed the sight of his parents, as the slave his torturer. Gentlemen of 30 or 40 years old, fitt for any employment in the common wealth, were to stand like greate mutes and fools bare headed before their Parents. . . ."[54]

When this hatred became "politicized," the social and political inferior was no longer seen as son or subject, servant or apprentice, but rather as the menacing "Many-Headed Monster." Perhaps only a country whose basic social institutions seem relatively stable and unthreatened, only an élite that believes itself relatively secure, can risk revolution. Regardless, that sense of security did not last. As Christopher Hill points out, the traditional fear of "the giddy-headed multitude" reasserted itself even before the politicized New Model Army and Leveller propaganda gave substance to those fears.[55] By the end of the century the fear of the Many-Headed Monster had taken on a new guise. In the later seventeenth century the condition of being masterless seems to have been widespread

and generally recognized—precisely the situation viewed so pessi-
mistically in the Hobbesian state of nature—and the poor, having
become mobile, are now seen, when acting against the interest of
the élite, as the mob. "The Nobility, Gentry and Scholars, as well as
most of the Merchants and chief Tradesmen," noted Edward
Chamberlayne at the beginning of Queen Anne's reign, "are
extreamely well polished in their behavior; but the common sort
are rude and even barbarous, as the effects of popular Tumults
(which are here called the Mobile) shews, who when they are got
together, comit the greatest outrages. . . ."[56]

Whether or not there is anything in the notion that the political
nation could afford almost a century of intermittent conflict because social relations seemed relatively fixed or at least safe, there
can be no question about the unprecedented political instability
that marked the whole century before the 1720s. Place and
patronage were standard means by which early modern monar-
chies attempted to tie the fortunes of the political nation to their
own and to secure at least obedience and, if possible, active collab-
oration in the task of ruling the country. Almost twenty years ago
C. V. Wedgwood pointed out that it was a "cardinal weakness of
King Charles's government" that "he had no civil service, no country-wide bureaucratic class dependent on him."[57] G. E. Aylmer's
pioneering study of the Caroline bureaucracy carries the argument
several steps further: not only did Charles lack a country-wide class
of dependent local governors, his very control over his central
administration was compromised by rights to office, which he could
not touch, by divided loyalties, by the threat posed by any reform to
already existing interests. Instead of a bulwark of monarchy, the
bureaucracy, such as it was in 1640, was a burden on the country
sufficient to arouse the envy and resentment of the Parliamentary
classes, but neither cohesive nor powerful enough to offer any prop
to the tottering fortunes of the King.[58] War and the Interregnum
gave England a larger and considerably more efficient administration, to which the place bills, beginning in 1675, testify; but local
government remained in the hands of local élites, and Parliament
remained the arena for political conflict rather than the means by
which a strong executive obtained the consent of the political
nation for its legislative acts.[59] Rather than seeking to contain

politics within the comparatively safe confines of Westminster, opposition politicians from the beginning of the century sought to extend the conflict and to exploit local resources by expanding the electorate—the subject of J. H. Plumb's essay reprinted here. Eventually the trend was reversed; after 1714 a strong Whig executive took advantage of the vacuum left by the suicide of the Tory party and imposed a one-party regime in both the administration and Parliament. However, until those happy events, if indeed they were happy, volatility, if not always outright violence, characterized much of the political process.

It would be wrong to leave this sketch of some aspects of seventeenth-century England as though most major changes aborted: a population that ceased its rapid growth with significant consequences for both society and the economy; a rapid social mobility that ceased in mid-century and was followed by a half century in which the social structure hardened; a social conservatism that permitted patriarchalism to appear to remain a viable basis for familial as well as social and political authority, despite the erosion caused by contractual theories and relations; a growth of the political community given life by the expanding franchise, which aborted in Walpole's triumphant imposition of one-party rule.

When Marchamont Nedham claimed that "Interest Will Not Lie," and Pope wrote "That Reason, Passion answer one great aim / That true Self-Love and Social are the same," they were giving voice to a real revolution, even though the political revolution of the 1640s had long run its course.[60] Any respectable intellectual of the early Stuart period could and would have told Nedham and Pope that reason and passion did not speak with one voice, but on the contrary that the task of reason was to rule the passions lest "inordinate desires and upstart passions catch the government from Reason."[61] Further, no orthodox thinker at the beginning of the century would have accepted the paradox that the unrestrained pursuit of self-interest was conducive to the general good of all; rather, they stressed "how dangerous it is / For any man to press beyond the place / To which his birth, or means, or knowledge ties him."[62] Instead, the King was supposed to preside over a commonwealth all parts of which demonstrated "their dutious subject-tion . . . by their forwardnesse in cooperating with him."[63] How radically different was the world in which Henry St. John calmly explored party motives in 1710: "We supposed the Whigs to be the remains [of the Exclusionists and] to lean for support on the Presbyterians and other sectaries, on the Bank and other corporations, on the Dutch and other allies."[64] The co-operative commonwealth had given way to sectional interests competing for power in the cockpit of Parliamentary politics, a development no longer to be bemoaned but rather simply to be analyzed and understood.

INTRODUCTION

1. See, *e.g.*, Trevor Aston, ed., *Crisis in Europe 1560–1660* (London, 1965); Lawrence Stone, ed., *Social Change and Revolution in England 1540–1640* (London, 1965); E. W. Ives, ed., *The English Revolution 1600–1660* (London, 1968); R. H. Parry, ed., *The English Civil War and After 1642–1658* (London, 1970); G. E. Aylmer, ed., *The Interregnum: The Quest for Settlement 1646–1660* (London, 1972); and Conrad Russell, ed., *The Origins of the English Civil War* (London, 1973).

2. At this writing Brian Manning's *Politics, Religion and the English Civil War* (London, 1973), has been announced but not published.

3. The increased complexity and subtlety of one Marxist view may be seen by comparing Christopher Hill, *The English Revolution, 1640* (London, 1940), with the same author's textbook of two decades later: *Century of Revolution, 1603–1714* (London, 1961), and there is no reason to suppose that the latter represents this fertile historian's final word on the subject. For what Lawrence Stone has fairly called a "neo-Marxist" interpretation, see Barrington Moore, Jr., *Social Origins of Dictatorship and Democracy* (Boston, 1966).

4. *The Gentry, 1540–1640, Economic History Review,* Supplement No. 1 (1953); "The General Crisis of the Seventeenth Century," *Past and Present,* 16 (1959), reprinted in Trevor Aston, ed., *Crisis in Europe 1560–1660* (London, 1965), pp. 63–102. "Revolution of despair" is Lawrence Stone's apt term: see his review of Perez Zagorin's *The Court and the Country* in *The New York Review of Books,* April 23, 1970, p. 41.

5. It was "not the brisk hard-bitten gentry of Professor Tawney, nor yet the moldy flea-bitten mere gentry of Professor Trevor-Roper" but "the rich gentry of England [who] organized themselves to oppose the activities of the king during the most severe constitutional crisis in English history." J. H. Hexter, "Storm over the Gentry," in *Reappraisals in History* (Northwestern University Press, 1961), p. 148.

6. See Christopher Hill, *Reformation to Industrial Revolution* (New York, 1967).

7. *The Causes of the English Revolution* (London, 1972), pp. 146–147.

8. *Modern Historians on British History 1485–1945. A Critical Bibliography 1945–1969* (London, 1970), p. 51.

9. The "Forward" to J. H. Hexter, *Reappraisals in History,* p. ix.

10. C. H. George, "The Making of the English Bourgeoisie," *Science and Society*, 35 (1971), p. 386.

11. Peter Laslett, *The World We Have Lost*, 2nd edition (London, 1971), p. 165.

12. Sir John Oglander, *A Royalist Notebook*, ed. Francis Bamford (New York, 1971), p. 109. G. E. Aylmer, ed., *The Interregnum* (London, 1972), pp. 25, 26.

13. Stone's quoted remarks come from a review published in *The New York Review of Books*, April 23, 1970, p. 41.

14. "The Process of Modernization and the Industrial Revolution in England," *Journal of Interdisciplinary History*, 3 (1972), 225–259.

15. See Lacy Baldwin Smith, " 'Christ, What a Fright'; The Tudor Portrait As an Icon," *Journal of Interdisciplinary History*, 4 (1973), 119–127.

16. J. P. Kenyon, *Robert Spencer, Earl of Sunderland, 1641-1702* (London, 1958), p. 7.

17. Thomas Sprat, as quoted in S. L. Bethell, *The Cultural Revolution of the Seventeenth Century* (London, 1951), p. 101.

18. James I, speech to Parliament, 21 March 1610: J. P. Kenyon, *The Stuart Constitution* (Cambridge, 1966), pp. 12–13.

19. Sir William Petty, *Political Arithmetic* (London, 1690), reprinted in *Later Stuart Tracts*, intro. George A. Aitken (New York, n.d.), p. 7.

20. Daniel Defoe, *A Tour Thro' the Whole Island of Great Britain* (London, 1724–26; Reprints of Economic Classics, New York, 1968), II, 602. For age distribution, see Peter Laslett, *The World We Have Lost*, 2nd ed. (London, 1971), p. 108; for occupational distribution, see L. A. Clarkson, *The Pre-Industrial Economy of England 1500–1750* (London, 1971), pp. 88–91.

21. Clarkson, *Pre-Industrial Economy of England*, pp. 106–108.

22. Laslett, *World We Have Lost*, p. 97.

23. As quoted in J. D. Chambers, *Population, Economy, and Society in Pre-Industrial England* (Oxford, 1972), p. 135.

24. *Ibid.*, p. 85.

25. E. A. Wrigley, "Family Limitation in Pre-Industrial England," *Economic History Review*, 2nd s., 19 (1966), 87.

26. *Ibid.*, pp. 93, 97.

27. E. H. Phelps Brown and Sheila V. Hopkins, "Seven Centuries of the Prices of Consumables, Compared with Builders' Wage Rates," *Economica*, n.s., 23 (1956), reprinted in *Essays in Economic History*, ed. E. M. Carus-Wilson (London, 1962), II, 179–196.

28. See Eric Kerridge, "The Movement of Rent, 1540–1640," *Economic History Review*, 2nd s., 6 (1953) reprinted in Carus-Wilson, *Essays in Economic History*, II, 208–226.

29. William Harrison, *The Description of England*, ed. Georges Edelen (Ithaca, N.Y., 1968), pp. 197–202; W. G. Hoskins, "The Rebuilding of Rural England, 1570–1640," *Past and Present*, 4 (1953), reprinted in *Provincial England: Essays in Economic and Social History* (London, 1963), pp. 131–148.

30. Eric Kerridge, *The Agricultural Revolution* (London, 1967), p. 328.

31. For the GNP estimate, see Clarkson, *Pre-Industrial Economy of England*, p. 130; Ralph Davis, *English Overseas Trade 1500–1700* (London, 1973), p. 8.

32. Davis, *English Overseas Trade*, pp. 55–56.

33. Christopher Wase, *Considerations concerning Free Schools* (Oxford, 1678), p. 13, as quoted in Lawrence Stone, "Literacy and Education in England, 1640–1900," *Past and Present*, 42 (1969), 72.

34. W. A. Speck, "Social Status in Late Stuart England," *Past and Present*, 34 (1966), 128–129.

35. Alan Everitt, *Change in the Provinces: the Seventeenth Century* (Leicester, 1969), pp. 8–11.

36. Lawrence Stone, *The Causes of the English Revolution 1529–1642* (London, 1972), p. 110; Everitt, *Change in the Provinces*, p. 13.

37. J. Cornwall, "The Early Tudor Gentry," *Economic History Review*, 2nd s., 17 (1964), 460; Laslett, *World We Have Lost*, pp. 64–65.

38. Everitt, *Change in the Provinces*, p. 22.

39. *The Agrarian History of England and Wales*, Vol. IV, *1500–1640*, ed. Joan Thirsk (Cambridge, 1967), p. 93.

40. F. J. Fisher, "London as an 'Engine of Economic Growth,' " *Britain and the Netherlands*, Vol. IV, eds. J. S. Bromley and E. H. Kossman (The Hague, 1971), p. 3. See also E. A. Wrigley, "A Simple Model of London's Importance in Changing English Society and Economy 1650–1750," *Past and Present*, 37 (1967), 44–70.

41. As quoted in Christopher Hill, *Reformation to Industrial Revolution* (New York, 1967), p. 15.

42. Fisher, "London as an 'Engine of Economic Growth,' " pp. 7–15.

43. *Ibid.*, p. 14; Clarkson, *Pre-Industrial Economy of England*, p. 87.

44. J. D. Chambers, *Population, Economy, and Society in Pre-Industrial England* (Oxford, 1972), p. 143.

45. *Ibid.*, pp. 141–147.

46. Sir William Petty, *Political Arithmetic* (London, 1690), reprinted in *Later Stuart Tracts*, intro. George A. Aitken (New York, n.d.), p. 31; see also Keith Thomas, "Work and Leisure in Pre-Industrial Society," *Past and Present*, 29 (1964), 50–62.

47. E. P. Thompson, "Time, Work-Discipline, and Industrial Capitalism," *Past and Present*, 38 (1967), 73.

48. *Ibid.*, p. 71.

49. *Ibid.*, p. 87.

50. *Divers Crab-Tree Lectures* (1639), p. 126, as quoted in Thompson, *loc. cit.*, p. 72.

51. David Herlihy, "Three Patterns of Social Mobility in Medieval History," *Journal of Interdisciplinary History*, 3 (1973), 623.

52. Isaac Barrow, *Of Industry* (London, 1700), p. 119, as quoted in Richard B. Schlatter, *The Social Ideas of Religious Leaders, 1660–1688* (Oxford, 1940), pp. 108–109.

53. Richard Baxter, *A Christian Directory* (1673), II, 517, as quoted in Schlatter, *Social Ideas of Religious Leaders*, p. 5.

54. *Aubrey's Brief Lives*, ed. Oliver Lawson Dick (London, 1950), pp. xl–xli. For the persistence of patriarchalism, its effects on politics, and its base in the social structure and early conditioning of seventeenth-century Englishmen, see Gordon J. Schochet, "Patriarchalism, Politics and Mass Attitudes in Stuart England," *Historical Journal*, 12 (1969), 413–441.

55. Christopher Hill, "The Many-Headed Monster in Late Tudor and Early Stuart Political Thinking," *From Renaissance to Counter-Reformation*, ed. C. H. Carter (New York, 1965), 296–324. How politics appeared to the newly politicized multitude during the revolutionary decades has been explored by Hill in "The Norman Yoke," *Puritanism and Revolution* (London, 1958), 50–122, and more generally in *The World Turned Upside Down* (London, 1973); see also Brian Manning, "The Outbreak of the English Civil War," *The English Civil War and After 1642–1658*, ed. R. H. Parry (London, 1970), 1–21.

56. Edward Chamberlayne, *Angliae Notitia* (20th ed., 1702), pp. 318–319, as quoted in Max Beloff, *Public Order and Popular Disturbances* (London, 1963), p. 9.

57. C. V. Wedgwood, "The Causes of the English Civil War," *History Today*, 5 (1955), 671.

58. G. E. Aylmer, "Office Holding as a Factor in English History," *History*, 44 (1959), 228–240, and *The King's Servants: The Civil Service of Charles I, 1625–42* (London, 1961).

59. J. H. Plumb, *The Growth of Political Stability in England, 1675–1725* (London, 1967), pp. 19, 48.

60. Quoted in C. H. George, "The Making of the English Bourgeoisie," *Science and Society*, 35 (1971), 385–414; see also J. A. W. Gunn, " 'Interest will not lie': a seventeenth-century political maxim," *Journal of the History of Ideas*, 29 (1968), 551–564.

61. John Milton, *Paradise Lost*, xii, 86–89, as quoted in W. H. Greenleaf, *Order, Empiricism and Politics* (London, 1964), p. 26.

62. George Chapman, *The Revenge of Bussy D'Ambois*, III, iv, 48–50, as quoted in Greenleaf, *Order, Empiricism and Politics*, p. 31.

63. Edward Forset, *A Comparative Discourse of the Bodies Natural and Politique* (London, 1606), pp. 17-18, quoated in Greenleaf, *Order, Empiricism and Politics*, p. 30.

64. Henry St. John, Viscount Bolingbroke, *A Letter to Sir William Windham* (1753), pp. 19–22, in *The Divided Society: Parties and Politics in England 1694–1716*, eds., G. S. Holmes and W. A. Speck (London, 1968), p. 142.

We are apt to think of traditional societies as relatively static, and of early modern England as a traditional, pre-industrial society. Lawrence Stone's pioneering study suggests that English society was more dynamic in the century before 1640 than in the century after that date, that not only did/individuals find greater opportunities to change their status but occupational and status groups changed their position relative to each other, so that the social landscape by 1700 presented quite a different picture from that of Tudor England. This essay both describes the change and attempts to analyze its causes and assess its consequences. Much of the analysis is arguable and many of the conclusions remain open to question, but only a powerful historical imagination could encompass so much of what is known about early modern English society in a single, if complex, synthesis, while disguising neither the weak points in the evidence nor the many questions that remain to be answered.

Lawrence Stone, who has been Dodge Professor of History at Princeton since 1963, was trained at Oxford and was a Fellow of Wadham College from 1950 to 1963. He has published on medieval English sculpture as well as on early modern English social history. His work ranges from major studies based on extensive archival research, such as the monumental The Crisis of the Aristocracy, 1558–1641 *(Oxford, 1965), to highly synthetic but no less valuable studies, such as the three articles collected in* The Causes of the English Revolution 1529–1642 *(London, 1972). The present article originally appeared in Past and Present, 33 (1966), 16–55, and is reprinted by permission of the author and of the Past and Present Society, Corpus Christi College, Oxford, which holds the world copyright.*

Social Mobility in England, 1500–1700*

Lawrence Stone

The purpose of this paper is fourfold: firstly, to sketch the configuration of a Western traditional society at a fairly advanced stage of its development, a model that might be applicable to any European society from the sixteenth to the eighteenth centuries; secondly, to produce the evidence for believing that between 1540 and 1640 English society experienced a seismic upheaval of un-. precedented magnitude; thirdly, to postulate some reasons both for the development of this upheaval and for its termination; and fourthly, to speculate about the political and religious conse- quences. The paper attempts—perhaps rashly—to take a broad overview of the society as a whole, and therefore ignores the important local variations which undoubtedly existed.

I MODELS

The first problem is what sort of a visual image we have of this early modern English society. Sociologists tend to describe pre- industrial societies in terms of a stepped pyramid, the lower classes forming the bottom step, and the aristocracy or plutocracy the apex (because of the erosion of the poor and the growth of the middle-class in contemporary Western society, it has turned into a

---

*Some of the many errors of sense and logic in early drafts of this paper were pointed out to me by David Bien, Christopher Hill, Michael Walzer, Jerrold Seigel, John Shy, and Joan Thirsk. Daniel Baugh went to great trouble in helping me to guess at the number of office-holders. I am very grateful to them for their assistance. An earlier version of this article was circulated for the 1965 Past and Present Annual Conference.

stepped lozenge). But one may reasonably doubt whether this model fits a traditional pre-industrial society. Two alternatives present themselves. The first—let us call it the United Nations model—is a tall skyscraper erected on top of a vast low podium. Within the podium, which extends over many acres, live 95 percent or more of the population, who are free to move along wide corridors and to rise and descend very shallow staircases within this limited level. The skyscraper itself, within which dwell the remaining 5 percent or less, is composed of a series of floors for status groups based on the ownership of land. Within it is a single infrequent elevator which always goes down with a full load of failures and superfluous younger sons, but often rises half empty. Around the skyscraper itself, however, there wind several ascending ramps, labelled Church, Law, Commerce, and Office. Some people camp out on the ramps, but it is draughty and wet out there, and most of them struggle upwards and then take shelter inside at the highest floor they can comfortably reach.

The second—the San Gimignano model—is a series of vertical towers upon a hill. In this model the hill represents the amorphous mass of the poor and the humble, and the towers a series of more or less independent economic and status hierarchies with their own internal elevators: land, church, law, commerce, and government office are the most conspicuous of these towers.

Neither of these models exactly fits the observed facts, but both are an improvement on the conventional stepped pyramid image. It will be argued in this paper that between 1500 and 1700 English society was moving from the United Nations towards the San Gimignano model as the status of business and the professions rose in the eyes of the landed classes.

II CATEGORIES
The Hierarchy of Status
In the sixteenth century there was a status hierarchy, not the loose competitive status agglomerations to which we are accustomed today.[1] Though there existed a few completely non-integrated groups—artists and stage-players, for example—and four semi-independent occupational hierarchies, the vast mass of the population was fitted into a single hierarchy of status defined by

titular rank, and to a certain extent by legal and fiscal privilege. The most fundamental dichotomy within the society was between the gentleman and the non-gentleman, a division that was based essentially upon the distinction between those who did, and those who did not, have to work with their hands. This is a critical division in all societies where human labour is the principal power-unit, apart from the horse and the ox, wind and water. The more extreme conservatives, heralds and others, argued that it took three generations for a family to purge its blood from the taint of inferiority and to become an accepted member of this upper class. In practice such notions seem to have had little effect, but the fact that they could be seriously propounded is evidence that an element of caste theory was to be found in Tudor England.

Within the dual system of gentlemen and non-gentlemen contemporaries recognized a rough sixfold status division:

GROUP 1.   The dependents on charity, whether widows, aged, or unemployed; also the apprentices and living-in servants, domestic, agricultural, or industrial, who composed as much as 15 percent to 25 percent of the adult male population.[2]

GROUP 2.   The living-out labourers, both rural and urban, agricultural and industrial.

GROUP 3.   The husbandmen, the lesser yeomen (both tenants and freeholders), and the more substantial yeomen; also the artisans, shopkeepers, and small internal traders.

GROUP 4.   The lesser, or parish, gentry.

GROUP 5.   The county élite: squires, knights, and baronets.

GROUP 6.   The peers: barons, viscounts, earls, marquises, and dukes.

This sixfold status hierarchy is based on the values of a primitive rural society. At the lower levels of groups 1–3 there already existed two parallel hierarchies for urban and rural society, but they can be roughly matched without too much difficulty. But both contemporaries and ourselves are faced with the more vexing problem of fitting into this scheme four semi-independent occupational hierarchies, whose precise relationship to the basic reference groupings was never fully clarified. These were:

GROUP A.   THE MERCHANTS.   The middling and large-scale exporters of London, Exeter, Bristol, Hull, and Newcastle, the wholesalers, the large retailers of the main cities, the customs farmers and government contractors, and the financiers of London. In the sixteenth and early seventeenth centuries they were still regarded in many quarters as distinctly inferior in status to a gentleman. As late as 1669, Edward Chamberlayne stated flatly that "Tradesmen in all ages and nations have been reputed ignoble," and a generation earlier there had been a brisk pamphlet discussion whether or not a gentleman's son lost his gentle status by becoming an apprentice. Because of this attitude the merchants were a mobile group of transients, very many of whom moved into and out of the group in a single lifetime, and nearly all in two generations; as a contemporary put it at the time, merchants "do attain to great wealth and riches, which for the most part they employ in purchasing land and little by little they do creep and seek to be gentlemen." In other words, the most successful tended to merge into groups 4 and 5.[3]

GROUP B. THE LAWYERS. These ranged all the way from the local attorney and solicitor to grandees like the Master of the Rolls and the Lord Chancellor. Over three quarters of those trained at the Inns of Court, that is the barristers and above, were of gentry or clergy stock, but we know little about the social origins, economic prospects, or accepted status of the local attorneys.[4]

GROUP C. THE CLERGY. These ranged in income and position from the curate to the archbishop, and varied in social origin from the copyholder to the squire. Even in a prosperous and socially and intellectually advanced area like Oxfordshire or Worcestershire, between three quarters and two thirds of the early seventeenth-century parish clergy were still of non-gentry origin. Though most rectors were comfortably off, and though the overall average real income probably remained much the same, substantial numbers of vicars and curates were existing on an income hardly different from that of unskilled labourers.[5] The higher clergy were ruthlessly plundered under the Tudors, and their social origins were generally inferior to those of the lawyers. For example, of twenty-eight bishops in the 1630s, the fathers of only nine were gentry; eight were clergymen, seven were merchants, one was a yeoman, and three were artisans or below.[6] It seems that the highest ranks of the clergy were generally regarded as inferior in status to the highest ranks of the legal profession, despite the presence of the former in the House of Lords. The precise reason for this lowly status is hard to determine. Was it the vigorous and widespread anti-clericalism of the age which both lowered respect for the profession and frightened off prospective entrants of gentry stock? Or the lack of assured tenure during a period of theological upheaval? Or the substantially reduced financial rewards to be expected even from a successful career? We do not know, but it is probable that all three factors interacted one upon the other.

GROUP D.   THE ADMINISTRATORS.   These are the office-holders in the royal household, the major departments of state, and the army and navy, men to whom administration was a professional life commitment. This definition includes all those dealt with by Professor Aylmer in *The King's Servants* except the courtiers at the apex of the system. By the early seventeenth century, these royal servants were predominantly of squirearchy or gentry origin, but with a substantial leavening from yeoman, merchant, and miscellaneous non-gentry stock.[7]

What we have, therefore, is a rural-based status hierarchy running from 1 to 6, the clarity and utility of which is marred by the existence of four occupational hierarchies, A, B, C, and D, whose exact positions within this standard system of reference were, and are, uncertain.

Moreover, it is unhappily true that 1, 2, and 3 include well over 90 percent of the population—perhaps as much as 95 percent—which means that a great deal of horizontal, and even some vertical, mobility within the vast mass of the population goes unrecognized. In such a society one cannot expect there to be very much upward mobility at the lower levels. Most of the population was living on the land, enjoying a very low income, and tied to the soil by the needs of manual labour for food production and distribution. A reasonable guess is that about 95 percent of the population was still rural in 1500, and about 85 percent in 1700.[8] Now in a society in which 90 percent of the population are manual workers on the land, even if every other job and office is filled by one of their sons, still only 11 percent can expect to change occupations.[9] Under such circumstances it is evident that the chances of upward economic mobility for the great majority of the population must be very small indeed.

The task of the historian of social mobility is complicated by a variety of difficulties. The degree to which a society appears open or closed both to contemporaries and to posterity depends partly on the prevailing myth, and partly on hard facts. For lack of anything better on which to base their judgements, historians tend to see a society much as the contemporaries saw it. Thus if seventeenth-century Englishmen and nineteenth-century Americans thought of their society as exceptionally mobile, then exceptionally mobile they appear in the history books. But there is also the social reality underlying the myth, a reality which cannot be too remote from the image without creating severe psychic tensions. The general contentment of the greater number is probably most strongly determined by the possibility of minor movement up and down at the lowest levels of groups 1, 2, and 3. But the quality of the society as it is seen by the historian is determined by two quite different factors. The first is the proportion of the lower and middling classes who are able to filter through into the élite: that is the number of ambitious youths who can move up from group 3 to group 4, the speed of acceptance of upwardly mobile elements of A, B, C, and D by 4 and 5, and the degree to which income, political power, and status are open to talent among 4, 5, and 6. The second factor is the method by which this filtration occurs. Is it "sponsored mobility" of youths selected for advancement at an early age, an upward movement planned and controlled by the existing élite for its own purpose of functional efficiency and the preservation of status lines? Or is it "contest mobility," the chance product of prolonged and open competitive struggle?[10]

The Hierarchy of Income

Tax data and other contemporary records suggest that the hierarchy of status corresponded roughly with the pyramid of incomes, and that the same was true within the four anomalous occupational categories of merchant, lawyer, official, and clergyman.[11] It should be noted that the spread of income distribution after taxation was enormous by modern standards, perhaps as many as 1,000 families enjoying a net income after tax of £1,000 a year or more, which was a hundred times greater than that of the unskilled labourer.

The Hierarchy of Power

Political power was rather less intimately linked to status than was income, but it was still close. Groups 3–6 and A, B, C, and D nearly all enjoyed the franchise, but in practice contests for seats in Parliament were fairly rare, and political affairs at the local level were run in towns exclusively by A and in the county by 5 and 6, with some support and occasional competition from elements of 4.[12] At the national level, power was exercised by courtiers and officials: that is, a select minority of groups 5 and 6, and the whole of group D.

At Court, a knight from the lower gentry like Sir Walter Raleigh ranked higher in status, wielded more power, and might even enjoy a larger income than a backwoods earl like Bath. But this top Court élite of politicians was too ephemeral in its composition and too amateur in its interests to be regarded as a permanent part of the official class.

III PATTERNS

The evidence is twofold, contemporary comment and statistics. The former is unreliable, firstly because what seems like great social mobility to contemporaries may appear very small to us; secondly because, when dealing with a small élite class, a numerically very small opening into it may seem gigantic to the élite but insignificant to the outsiders; and lastly because the individual example, which may be quite exceptional, cannot be used to prove a generalization. Finally, myth may not correspond to reality. The rags-to-riches legend of Dick Whittington may bear little relation to the actual life-prospects of an apprentice, although the fact that the legend first appears in 1605 may indicate growing aspiration for upward mobility.

There are three kinds of mobility, of which the first is the rise and fall of certain groups in relation to others. When studying this kind of change, it must be remembered that there are four elements in social stratification: the relative numbers, income, status, and political power of each group. It is very unlikely that the four will change together in perfect harmony and it may be necessary to construct four different profiles of mobility over time for each group.

The second consists of changes in the profile of stratification, that is to say in the distances between the groups: thus there can be yawning gulfs or barely perceptible cracks separating one social group from another in terms of income, status, or power; and the third consists of changes in the scale and range of individual mobility. This last, which is the one which usually attracts most attention but is historically in some ways the least important, has three variables: the direction, upwards or downwards; the height, that is to say the number of steps in the hierarchy to which the individual can climb or descend; and the frequency, the proportion of individuals in the group who are socially mobile.

Changes in Group Profiles

(1) NUMBERS. The great growth of population up to 1620, coupled with the continued engrossing of holdings by rich farmers, and heavy regressive taxation after 1642, must have caused a substantial increase in the size of groups 1 and 2 at the bottom of the heap, and an all too obvious growth of structural unemployment and under-employment which provoked the introduction of exceptional measures of poor relief and social control. Even in 1522-24 about one half of the population of Coventry, one third of that of Leicester and Exeter, and a substantially smaller proportion of the lesser country towns was reckoned to be below the poverty line, and therefore not taxable. In 1688, Gregory King estimated that over half the total population, rural and urban, earned less than was needed for subsistence. The late seventeenth-century Hearth Tax returns for one Midland village show 30 percent of all households below the tax level altogether, and a further 46 percent with only one hearth. In a town like Exeter conditions were even worse, with some 40 percent of households below the tax level.[13]

Secondly, there was a remarkable increase in the number of the upper classes, which trebled at a period when the total population barely doubled. The number of peers rose from 60 to 160; of baronets and knights from 500 to 1,400; of squires from perhaps

800 to 3,000; of armigerous gentry from perhaps 5,000 to around 15,000. This was due partly to the increase of land in private ownership, partly to the generation of new wealth in trade, the law, office and agriculture, and partly to the casual government attitude towards the inflation of honours.[14]

Thirdly, there were striking fluctuations in the numbers of the clergy. The profession contracted sharply—perhaps by 50 percent —with the elimination of the regular clergy at the Reformation and the subsequent plunder of the Church. In 1560, with no monks or chantry priests left, and perhaps as many as 2,000 of the 9,000 livings unfilled, the clergy were fewer in numbers than they had been for centuries. Thereafter numbers expanded again as vacant livings were filled, curacies increased, and a surplus of talented preachers were taken on as lecturers. The peak of the revival must have been in the 1640s, but the post-Restoration slump in both university education and religious enthusiasm, and the suppression of lecturers, must have cut the numbers back again.

The other professions showed sustained and striking increases in size. In particular the lawyers grew by leaps and bounds. The numbers called to the bar at the Inns of Court increased by over 40 percent between the 1590s and the 1630s. At the same time there were complaints about the proliferation of attorneys and solicitors. An official survey of 1633 stated that the number of attorneys enrolled in the court of Common Pleas had risen from 342 to 1,383 since 1578, and, in 1689, John Aubrey said it was thought that there were nearly 3,000 in England. In 1688, Gregory King reckoned the entire legal profession at 10,000.[15] In addition, the medical profession grew very rapidly, and there may have been as many as 1,000 doctors, surgeons, and apothecaries practicing medicine between 1603 and 1643.[16]

Though statistics are wholly lacking, it is likely that there was an equally important proliferation of secretarial and administrative jobs. The rise of literacy stimulated the rise of record-keeping, the rise of record-keeping the increase of record-keepers. An increasingly specialized society demanded ever more specialized services. The Court and central royal bureaucracy seems to have been stabilized at about 600 persons up to the Civil War, and showed only limited signs of increase in minor and unauthorized clerical

posts, while in the provinces there were about another 600 petty
and part-time officials. But the English Revolution—like all revolutions—demanded a great expansion of state employees, partly as
soldiers to hold down the defeated party and ward off external
threats, partly as officials to exact taxes to pay for the war, and to
handle the bold projects of social engineering that revolutionary
governments always embark upon. Much of this expansion survived the emergency, and Restoration England found itself sad-
dled with a large navy, a small standing army, and a new force of
excisemen, Hearth Tax collectors, Customs officers, Treasury
officials, and dockyard workers whose political role as obsequious
government supporters soon aroused the alarm of the Country
Party.

How far these new offices were an avenue of upward mobility is
uncertain but they certainly expanded enormously the numbers of
the professional and administrative classes during and after the
Civil War. By the late eighteenth century the number of these new
central offices enjoying fees and salaries of over £100 a year was
perhaps around 1,000, while those earning between £50 and
£100 ran into several thousands. As for local officers, nothing
whatever is known, but here again there must have been several
thousand of them. Although the major increase in the number of
officers occurred in the hundred years after the accession of
William III, there is still some reason to believe that there must
have been up to 3,000 or 4,000 local and central office-holders in
1690 with incomes over £100 and at least as many again with
incomes between £50 and £100.[17]

Perhaps equally important was the increase throughout the
whole of the sixteenth and seventeenth centuries in the numbers of
secretaries and agents of private landlords and businessmen.[18]
Lastly, it can hardly be doubted that urbanization and greater
commercial activity both at home and abroad must have caused a
very substantial increase in the numbers of merchants and
shopkeepers.

(2) INCOME. Throughout the sixteenth century the pressure of
excess supply of labour relative to demand not only increased
unemployment but also forced down real wages to an alarming
degree, the Phelps Brown index suggesting a decline by as much as

50 percent.[19] Even if this is an unduly pessimistic calculation, the fall was undoubtedly of a magnitude for which there is no parallel in English history since the thirteenth century. The living standards of the labouring classes went down sharply in the sixteenth century, and stayed down throughout the seventeenth. On the other hand, throughout the whole of the sixteenth century and much of the seventeenth there was a striking rise in the material comforts of all classes from yeomen upwards, groups who benefited from rising agricultural prices, increased commercial activity, and increased demand for professional services. This is shown by the increase in the amount of domestic equipment mentioned by William Harrison and others and proven by the study of probate inventories; and by the increased number of rooms in housing erected during what has been described as "The Great Rebuilding."[20] At the gentry level, there is some rough statistical evidence to suggest that the years 1575–1625 saw more country-house building than any other fifty-year period in our history,[21] which is itself significant proof of a "rise of the gentry."

It is probable, but not yet proven, that the average income and capital value of the London monopoly merchants and financiers rose considerably throughout the period.[22] The income of nobles and courtiers certainly fell sharply in the late sixteenth century but recovered in the early seventeenth.[23] And lastly the income of the higher clergy was sharply curtailed at and after the Reformation, the process only stopping at the accession of James I. Although the income of some of the lower clergy kept pace with prices, that of the others, particularly vicars and curates, probably fell.[24] We do not yet know enough about lawyers or administrators to reach a firm conclusion, although the impression is that their economic position was improving, as was certainly that of medical practitioners. It is an ill wind which blows nobody any good, and the increase of smallpox and venereal disease brought wealth to many doctors' pockets.[25]

For one hundred years after the Restoration, however, there is reason to believe that the fortunes of the various levels of the landed classes were dramatically reversed from the trends of the previous century. The holdings of the aristocracy and greater landlords steadily increased, those of the small yeomen and freeholders were converted into leaseholds, and the smaller gentry were economically depressed by the stagnation of food prices and the rise of taxation on the land.[26]

(3) STATUS.   After a severe slump in the sixteenth century, there was a marked rise in the middle of the seventeenth century in the status of the lesser clergy, as they became better educated, better paid, and of more genteel social origins;[27] secondly, there was an improvement in the status of lesser legal officials like country attorneys, culminating in the formation in 1739 of a professional organization, "The Society of Gentlemen Practisers";[28] thirdly, there was a rise in status of the medical profession as a whole as its professional and educational standards improved; and fourthly, there was a slow but steady rise in the standing of the merchant class in the eyes of the gentry. By the middle of the seventeenth century, the old view that the younger son of a gentleman lost his gentility by becoming an apprentice was still held only by a few legal pendants, heralds, and other social conservatives.

These changes were all the product of the upgrading of trade and the professions relative to the landed classes. What cannot at present be determined is whether this was a result of an influx of superfluous younger sons of gentry, who had to be provided for somehow or other; or whether the influx was the result not so much of economic necessity as of a change in attitude towards occupations whose utility to society as a whole was increasingly being recognized. The probability is that the ideological and the economic changes marched hand in hand, thus relieving the historian of the responsibility of distinguishing horse from cart.

Thirdly, at the upper levels there was a striking though temporary fall in the prestige of the peers in the early seventeenth century, demonstrated by a decline in tenant loyalty, gentry deference, and electoral obedience. This decline prepared the way for the abolition of the House of Lords in 1649.[29] And lastly there was a similar decline in the status of courtiers, as a "Country" interest and a "Country" morality, expressed in a "Country Party," emerged as a self-conscious interest group with a well-defined ideological content.[30]

(4) POWER.   In the sixteenth century, thanks to the growing strength of the Crown, there was a decline in the political authority

of peers; in the seventeenth century, thanks to the growing power of Parliament, there was a decline in the political influence of courtiers; the beneficiaries of both movements were the greater gentry, although the peers were recovering some of their power again towards the end of the century.[31] Secondly, the political influence of the clergy was virtually eliminated at the Reformation, 'a loss which was only partially and temporarily made up in the 1630s. And thirdly there was a marked increase in the influence of the merchant community over English policy—especially foreign policy—thanks to the leverage it could exercise over any government by the offer or withholding of its facilities for credit.

By dividing this analysis of changes in group profiles into four distinct sections, the two important shifts in English society have tended to be lost to view. The first was a polarization of society into rich and poor: the upper classes became relatively more numerous, and their real incomes rose; the poor became relatively more numerous and their real incomes fell. The second was a greater equality among the upper classes: firstly, the wealth and power of the greater gentry increased relative to those of the aristocracy; and secondly, members of the trades and professions rose in wealth, numbers, and social status relative to the landed classes. How far this last development has proceeded can be glimpsed by looking at Gregory King's not implausible guesses about the structure of society in 1688. He estimated that there were 10,000 merchants by land and sea, 10,000 clergy, 5,000 greater and 5,000 lesser officials, 10,000 lawyers, 16,000 persons in the sciences and liberal arts, and 9,000 army and navy officers, making 65,000 in all. When one considers that he reckoned there were only 16,000 gentlemen and above, plus 40,000 wealthier freeholders, and that (if his figures are to be trusted) the total income of the professional and commercial groups was now nearly as great as that of the landed proprietors, it becomes clear that English society no longer conformed to the traditional pattern.[32] The landed classes might continue to wield political power and be the arbiters of social status for another two hundred years, but they had now to temper the exercise of this authority with a careful regard for these newer elements in the society.

Changes in Individual Mobility

(1) HORIZONTAL.   Individual mobility may be horizontal from one geographical area or occupation to another, or vertical, up or down the social and economic scale. The two are interrelated in that although most people move horizontally to avoid slipping downwards, there are still some who do so in the hope of also moving vertically upwards. To the extent that horizontal mobility reflects the second motive rather than the first, therefore, it is an indicator of rising aspirations, though by no means necessarily of rising achievements.

(a) Internal.   There is good reason to suppose that physical mobility, even in the village, was far greater than is generally supposed. Both the muster rolls and the detailed census returns of two individual villages suggest a turnover as high as 50 percent to 60 percent in ten years. If removal by death accounted for some 20 percent, there are still some 30–40 percent who moved on in a given ten-year span, which indicates that the seventeenth-century village was very far from being a static or isolated unit.[33] This mobility can partly be explained by the high proportion of the community who worked as living-in servants. These would move away from home to take service and move on again to change employers or to get married. Partly it was caused by a steady process of buying and selling of small properties and engrossing of holdings. A good deal of it, however, was caused by two major trends. There was a movement from the more densely settled areas into undeveloped land in the forests, the fens, and the Highland zone; and there was perhaps an even more massive drift from the countryside to the towns, and especially London. The first movement is difficult to document statistically, but is evident from many local estate records.[34] Moreover there was a very great increase in the volume of food production over these two centuries, so great that England became a net exporter of corn on a very large scale by the end of the seventeenth century, despite the doubling of its population. This has to be explained mainly by the opening up of virgin lands by a restlessly mobile population seeking a living wherever opportunity offered.

The flow into the towns is more easily demonstrated. As one

would expect if the population doubled, most towns show some growth after 1550. In the early sixteenth century London had a population of about 60,000, there was one other town of more than 10,000, and not more than fourteen of more than 5,000. Between 1550 and 1650 a few places like Norwich, Newcastle, York, and Bristol may have doubled or trebled to between 12,000 and 20,000, but London and its suburbs increased sixfold to about 350,000. By now London was clearly in a class by itself, and it went on growing to about 550,000 by the end of the century. In other words, London comprised perhaps 2 percent of the population of England and Wales in 1500, 5 percent in 1600, and 10 percent in 1700. In view of the very high urban death rates, this massive increase is evidence that a large proportion of the surplus population in the countryside was annually pouring into the capital city. Even when the city was devastated by plague and lost some 15 percent of its inhabitants, as occurred in 1603 and 1625, so great was the influx that the losses were made up within two years, to judge from the statistics of baptisms, marriages, and burials.[35] A London parson in the reign of Elizabeth remarked that every twelve years or so "the most part of the parish changeth, as I by experience know, some goinge and some comminge"—a situation which resembles nothing so much as Los Angeles in the mid-twentieth century.[36] What effect this enormous shift of population had upon status or living standards is entirely unknown, but it may well have been downward on both counts. Many of these wanderers failed to find a permanent home either on the wastes and forests or in the towns, and there is plenty of evidence—if of a non-quantitative character—for a serious increase of vagabondage.

One rung up the social ladder, however, horizontal mobility was probably more rewarding. It was certainly so for craftsmen trained in a skill through the expensive and tedious process of apprenticeship, for the Hearth Tax returns indicate that the income of the urban craftsman was a good deal higher than that of his rural counterpart.[37] In this connection some interesting conclusions emerge from an analysis of the apprenticeship records of London companies. These show that between the early sixteenth and the early eighteenth centuries there was a striking change in the geographical distribution of recruitment. Professor Thrupp had noted that in the late fifteenth century nearly half the apprentices of two London companies had come from the north, and there is evidence that this pattern persisted for another hundred years. The only early sixteenth-century records are what survives of the list of men who had completed their apprenticeships and were admitted to the Freedom of the City, mostly between 1535 and 1553. They show that over half came from north and west of a line Trent-Severn-Bournemouth. The pattern is confirmed by the later records of apprenticeship in the Carpenters' and Fishmongers' Companies. Both recruited about 40 percent from the Highland zone up to the Civil War, but only 20 percent or less by the end of the seventeenth century. There was a corresponding rise of apprentices from London and the four home counties from less than 20 percent before the Civil War to well over 50 percent by 1700, rising to 70 percent or more by 1750. This contraction of the area of recruitment receives striking confirmation from the records of the Cutlers' Company at Sheffield, which show that recruits from over thirty-one miles away fell from 22 percent to 5 percent between the second and the fourth quarter of the seventeenth century and did not rise above 12 percent for another hundred years. The second important trend over these years was from sons of agricultural workers and smallholders—yeomen, husbandmen, and labourers—to the sons of artisans and small tradesmen. This movement was most intense in the late seventeenth century, the proportion of sons of artisans among apprentices rising from 50 percent to 74 percent in the Carpenters' Company between 1654 and 1693, and from 39 percent to 63 percent in the Fishmongers' Company between 1641 and 1704.[38]

Just what these two movements mean is not entirely clear. These apprentices were a fortunate élite who were only a tiny minority of the mass of migrants to London and only about a third of whom were destined to stay and become Freemen of the City after their apprenticeship had expired. But the startling decline of immigrants from the north and west, and the almost equally impressive rise in the proportion of sons of artisans, surely indicate a closing of both horizontal and occupational mobility channels. Why this should be so we do not know. Was it due to changing opportunities for employment in the north and west, or to declining attraction of apprenticeship in London; or was it the automatic product of the expansion of numbers of both artisans in general and Londoners in particular, which made internal recruitment more possible? Whatever the cause, it is clear that a phase of very active horizontal mobility both in geographical range and in occupational shift was replaced by conditions of relative quiescence.

(b) External.   Between 1620 and 1640 some 80,000 Englishmen emigrated to America and the West Indies. Those who survived the first harsh years in America received very much greater land than they could ever hope for at home, and there is evidence to suggest that for the humble the move involved some general but modest upward status (and perhaps also economic) mobility.[39] Mid-seventeenth-century Massachusetts was a rural society of small yeomen farmers, without either landed gentry above or landless poor below.[40]

Far more significant mobility was achieved by colonial exploitation of Ireland. Those who entered the Irish scene in the 1590s obtained rich pickings in land grants and government offices—and lived to profit by the economic growth of the early seventeenth century—found themselves endowed with great wealth which was easily converted into status by the purchase of an Irish title. The richest man in England in 1640 was almost certainly Robert Boyle, Earl of Cork, who had landed in Dublin fifty-two years before as a penniless adventurer.[41] By emigration in the seventeenth century, whether to Ireland, or to America, or to the West Indies, horizontal mobility often became a means of moving upwards.

(2) VERTICAL

(a) Upward (economic and status).   The basic evidence to support the hypothesis that this period saw a phase of unprecedented individual mobility, upwards and downwards, followed by a fresh period of stability, lies in the statistics for the purchase and sale of land. They rise to a peak in the 1610s, 250 percent higher than in the 1560s. This great movement had spent itself before the Civil War, and land transfers had begun to slow up after 1620. By 1700 the land market was once again almost as tight as it had been in the early sixteenth century.[42]

For those who were not gentlemen there were various ways of moving upwards. University education on a scholarship, followed by entry into the church, certainly led to improvement in status, but only in the late seventeenth century did it normally lead to a reasonably well-paid or secure position.[43] Shrewd manipulation of the land and the agricultural produce market was far more important: the social and economic rise of many yeomen into the lesser gentry was a well-established feature of the society, at any rate before rents began rising steeply in the early seventeenth century.[44] Success in the servicing and retail trades offered some limited opportunity for self-improvement, though this was rarely the road to substantial wealth and power. Service as agent or steward of a large landed estate sometimes brought both status and financial rewards.[45] Apprenticeship to a leading merchant was a common way to rise quite high in the social scale. Commerce was the origin of the family wealth of two out of the fourteen richest Yorkshire squires in 1642, one out of twenty-five leading Somerset squires in the 1630s, 7 percent of the Early Stuart baronetage, and 4 percent of the new Early Stuart peerage. These figures suggest that both contemporaries and posterity have exaggerated the scale of the movement, but how it compared with earlier or later periods we do not know.[46]

As for the post-Restoration period, the remarkable commercial expansion of the late seventeenth century clearly created a great deal of new wealth. What is not so certain, however, is how it was distributed. Was it concentrated in the hands of a few men like Sir Josiah Child and Sir John Banks, or was it spread over the mercantile community as a whole? The closing down of the land market suggests that, however it was distributed, less of this wealth than before was being converted into social status by the purchase of an estate, and more of it was being reinvested in long-term mortgages, commerce, and banking.[47] Thus neither the expansion of the bureaucracy nor the expansion of trade are incompatible with the hypothesis of an increasingly immobile society.

For a young man of gentle birth, the fastest ways of moving up the social scale were the lotteries of marriage with an heiress, Court favour, and success at the law. The first of the three is usually neglected or ignored by social historians, but it was probably the commonest method of upward movement for gentlemen. The second, which was only open to a tiny handful of the horde of aspirants, could lead to dizzy heights of wealth and grandeur—witness the careers of the Earl of Leicester under Elizabeth, and the Duke of Buckingham under James. An analysis of the available evidence suggests that royal bounty reached a peak in the reign of James and then declined. The top positions in the law were also very rewarding in terms of wealth and status, but we have no way of telling what changes occurred over time in the numbers who benefited or the amount of profit they realized. Lastly the commonest, but certainly the slowest, of all the status elevators was thrift and diligence in estate management, a force which carried many gentry upwards into the squirearchy, and one or two squires upwards into the peerage.[48] It is worth noting that if we substitute India for Ireland, these avenues of upward mobility are precisely those operating a hundred years later in the middle of the eighteenth century: four fast elevators: marriage, the law, high government service, and the colonies; three medium fast: trade, government contracting, and finance; and two slow: estate management and professions other than the law.[49]

(b) Downward (economic and status). Downward mobility was the lot of those who were improvident or incompetent, extravagant or unlucky. History, however, rarely records, and even more rarely pays attention to, such tragedies. The victims sink without trace or comment. The fact that they were extremely common between 1560 and 1640 is proven by the dizzy rise of land sales up to 1620, before the other factors came into play to reduce again the likelihood of ruin and to shut off the supply of land for the market.

The final question to which no firm answer can be given, is the degree of stability achieved by the socially and economically mobile at this period. Plenty of examples can be instanced of wasteful and dissolute sons of self-made men who ran through the fortune accumulated by their fathers and so reduced the family to the status from which it began. And it may well be that the status-seeker of the Tudor age experienced considerable difficulty in founding a family that would last. But when the land market closed down in the late seventeenth century, when the pressure of demographic growth and price revolution eased off, when the strict settlement made alienation of property extremely difficult, when institutional road blocks had been erected to confine power to the

existing élite, then it may well be that families were established
which were capable of withstanding for generations all but the
ineluctable processes of biological failure in the male line. Professor Tawney discovered that in ten counties one third of all manors
changed hands by purchase and sale at least once every forty years
between 1561 and 1640. He also found that of sixty-two large
landowning families in the area in 1640, over half were still large
landowners in 1874.[50] These two pieces of evidence put together
suggest that those who rose in the social scale in the early seventeenth century, towards the end of the great phase of mobility, had
a good chance of establishing their family on the new level of
income and status once the avenues of mobility were closed.
Indeed, it may have been just these social climbers who were most
anxious to slam the door behind them, a suggestion which is
supported by the socially very exclusive marriage patterns of the
children of the newly risen Henrician and Jacobean peers in the
mid-sixteenth and mid-seventeenth centuries.[51]

The argument that the period 1560–1640 was an exceptionally
mobile one depends upon the statistical evidence, but it is also
supported by the weight of contemporary comment running from
Thomas Fuller, William Habington, and Robert Reyce to the
playwrights like Marston and Massinger. In 1665, Edward Waterhouse published his *Gentleman's Monitor, or a sober Inspection into the
Virtue, Vices and ordinary means of the rise and decay of men and
families.* Though not a very profound analysis, and though sloppily
organized, so far as I know this is the first full-scale study of social
mobility ever to have been attempted in Europe, and possibly in the
world. It is surely no mere coincidence that Waterhouse should
have written at the end of this period of maximum upheaval.

IV CAUSES

Universal Factors

We have very little precise data about social mobility in traditional societies. All we do know is firstly that before the nineteenth
century towns failed to reproduce themselves because of the high
wastage rate from disease, and that as a result there is bound to be a
good deal of horizontal mobility from rural to urban areas if town
life is to survive at all.[52] Secondly we know that the random

distribution of sterility and intelligence (or lack of it) creates some vertical mobility in all societies, however highly stratified and caste-ridden they may be. There is a high probability that any one family over a period of one or two hundred years will fail in the direct male line; there is also the certainty that the distribution of inherited intelligence and stupidity will not conform to the existing status hierarchy and that inequality of opportunity cannot always prevent consequential mobility upwards or downwards. Thirdly we know that in all societies the most promising avenues of upward mobility, apart from the lottery of marriage, are through occupational groups A, B, C, and D. Both the amount and the range of this mobility will depend partly on the psychological attitudes of the entrants into these occupations (whether they are active risk-taking entrepreneurs, or cautious conservatives with limited ambitions); partly on major long-term changes in the demands by society for their services; and partly on changes in the legal and psychological obstacles to assimilation into the élite of the upwardly mobile. If this is the normal situation, there were certain peculiar features operating in sixteenth- and seventeenth-century England that gave English mobility its special character, and dictated the remarkable changes that took place over these two hundred years.

Factors Particular to Early Modern England

(1) PRIMOGENITURE.   In all the upper ranks of society primogeniture was the rule.[53] Eldest sons usually inherited the great bulk of the estates of peers, gentry, and yeoman farmers. Moreover, eldest sons received a better and longer education, and were better placed to obtain rich wives and good jobs at Court and in government, thanks to the more energetic patronage of their fathers. Their life chances therefore were very good. In the sixteenth century younger sons were often left small landed estates, either in outright gift or for life or lives, but by the seventeenth century they could normally expect no more than a modest life annuity which expired at their death. They were therefore downwardly mobile from the very beginning of their careers, and were obliged to feed into the professional and business groups if they were to make their way in the world. If they failed, their children were liable to sink still further down the scale and disappear into the great mass of

labourers and small tradesmen. Examples can be found of this downward process, but the paucity of evidence makes it virtually impossible to demonstrate the trend in statistical terms.

(2) FAMILY PATTERNS. Much more research is needed on this subject, but, so far as we can tell, marriages were arranged by parents with an eye to material advantage. At the upper levels among the heirs male there was relatively little interstratal marriage, although great wealth could often buy a socially good marriage for a daughter: thus between 1600 and 1659 some 4 percent of all marriages of peers were to the daughters or widows of aldermen. Some two thirds of the younger sons and daughters of peers were obliged to marry below them, presumably mostly into the squirearchy. At the lower levels of society, we know virtually nothing about marriage, and until some such study as Charles Tilly has just published on the Vendée has been completed, our ignorance will remain.[54]

The two main requirements for upward mobility—capital and patronage—both hinged on the family. At a time when the interest rate was 10 percent and long-term credit hard to come by, the easiest road to riches was through inheritance or marriage: for example some 8 percent of London Jacobean aldermen had, when apprentices, married their master's daughter, while several of the richest merchants of Elizabethan Exeter had got a start by capturing the fancy of a rich widow.[55] Similarly family connections usually provided the initial leverage to get a man started on a career in this deferential society where success hinged on patronage, as is well exemplified in the case of Pepys.

(3) THE VALUE SYSTEM. Societies are profoundly affected by the way people think of themselves, regardless of objective criteria such as wealth. The most important aspects of sixteenth- and seventeenth-century thinking which affected social mobility were:

(a) The Great Chain of Being. The official theory, which was very widely accepted, was that everyone had his place in the social system and that it was his duty to stay in it. Both upward and downward mobility were deplored. This theory was clearly at variance with the facts and in the early seventeenth century there began to be heard more egalitarian ideas which culminated in the social and political thinking of the Levellers. These views were egalitarian in that they expressed hostility to the concept of hierarchy, and a desire to reduce the distinctions that cut one group off from another: only the early Renaissance humanists had wished to preserve the hierarchy but to throw it open to talent. Both of these were minority opinions and the more common view was that the functional needs of a modern state could and should be matched to the traditional hierarchy of birth by educating each social group to meet its inherited responsibilities. This re-vamping of medieval social ideals to fit the new political conditions led to an intensification of hostility towards social mobility, which was at the same time undoubtedly on the increase. There was a flood of laments about the decay of ancient families, there was widespread and embittered comment on the ostentatious upward mobility of the merchant class, and there was also a good deal of complaint that consumption standards and patterns of life no longer conformed to the ideal status hierarchy.[56] This criticism made it very difficult for the arriviste to achieve social acceptability in his own person, although it was usually easy enough for his son.

On the other hand, we shall see that these traditional views were undergoing considerable modification, and attitudes towards the professions were softening markedly by the middle of the seventeenth century. The decline of war and the church as the two major occupations for the upper classes, the rise in educational standards, the shift to an ideal of administrative and political service to the state or local community, the growing realization of the potentialities for upward mobility of trade and the professions, all led increasing numbers of the gentry class, both elder and younger sons, to seek an outlet for their energies in a career in the law and government office, and some in trade and medicine. For both functional and social reasons, the status of the professions was rising relatively to that of the landed classes, so that by the late seventeenth century the Church and the armed services were again becoming popular.

(b) Consumption as a test of status. All commentators stressed the obligation to maintain a suitable display as a mark of gentility or nobility. The cost of such displays rose under pressure from below, and there developed a double standard of consumption, that of the old feudal lord with open house and numerous servants in the

country, and that of the cultivated Maecenas at Court. Either could be ruinous, and those who tried to maintain both usually spent in excess of income. Excessive consumption was thus one of the principal causes of downward mobility,[57] and the obligation to spend to maintain status was a powerful brake on rapid upward economic mobility. At each stage the new rich had to pause and spend freely in order to establish themselves in their position in society.

Destabilizing Factors, 1540–1640

There was a whole series of strongly disruptive forces at work on society between 1540 and 1640, but which were not present to anything like the same degree before or after.

(1) DEMOGRAPHIC GROWTH. Firm statistics are impossible to come by, but the best guess is that between 1500 and 1620 the population of England and Wales nearly doubled, from between 2.5 and 3 million to 5 million. This added enormously to the labour force and caused horizontal mobility and urbanization. After 1620, however, there is every sign that, except perhaps in the north-west, plague, land hunger, commercial difficulties, family limitation, and emigration combined to reduce the increase to far more modest proportions.[58]

(2) DIFFERENTIAL FERTILITY. Between 1500 and 1630 there was almost certainly a differential fertility pattern by which the upper classes produced more children than the poor—the exact opposite of today. Thus an Elizabethan census of some 450 poor families with children in Norwich shows an average of 2.2 children per household, against between 4.25 and 4.7 children per household of well-to-do merchants of Norwich and Exeter. In the countryside the same discrepancy emerges from such data as are available.[59] The causes of this striking difference are not hard to find.

(a) There was a difference in the average age, duration, and frequency of marriage. For the eldest sons of peers (and probably also of squires) in the late sixteenth century, the average age of marriage (of those who did marry) was twenty-one, and for all children and grandchildren of peers, including both heirs male and younger sons, it was twenty-five to twenty-six. For yeomen and below, however, the average age of marriage in the early seventeenth century was twenty-seven to twenty-eight. Far more important for fertility is the age of marriage of women, and it is here that the contrast is most marked. Between 1550 and 1625 the daughters of the upper classes married at twenty to twenty-one, whereas daughters of the lower classes had to wait till they were twenty-four to twenty-five. The reproduction period of the latter was therefore significantly shorter than that of the former, and in the absence of contraception would have resulted in between one and two children fewer per family. The reasons for this pattern of delayed marriage among the lower classes are fairly clear. In the artisan class the seven-year apprenticeship system put a stop to marriage before the age of twenty-five or thereabouts; in the countryside most young people began as living-in servants for either domestic or agricultural work, while the eldest sons of freeholders or tenant farmers had to wait for the death of their father before they could afford to marry. This pattern determined the female age of marriage, since it seems to have been a convention from top to bottom of seventeenth-century society to marry women only about three years younger than oneself.[60]

Equally important in producing greater upper-class fertility was the very high rate of re-marriage at this level of society, so that the interruption of the procreative process by death of husband or wife (which was an extremely frequent occurrence) was reduced to a minimum. There is reason to believe that both marriage and re-marriage was less easy for those in less favourable economic circumstances, and indeed at Lichfield at the end of the seventeenth century as many as 31 percent of all women in the fertile age-group between twenty-five and forty-four were either widows or spinsters.[61]

(b) There was a difference in natural fertility: there is clear evidence that lactation impedes fertility, although the precise share of this effect between the physiological prevention of ovulation and a social taboo on sexual intercourse with a suckling woman is at present unknown.[62] Now in the upper classes infants were put out to lower-class wet-nurses at birth, whereas prolonged lactation by the mother for up to two years was normal among the poor.

(c) There was a difference in infant mortality: more upper-class children survived to a marriageable age, since the death rate among upper-class infants was almost certainly lower than among the poor. In one parish of the city of York in the healthy years 1572–85, children under the age of two made up 34 percent of all burials. The genealogical records of the peerage suggest a considerably lower rate, the expectation of life at birth at that period being about thirty-five for boys and thirty-eight for girls.[63] This was presumably because these children lived in the countryside rather than in towns, and were better housed, better clothed, and better fed (although they were admittedly exposed to the attentions of feckless wet-nurses and of doctors, who often did more harm than good). Moreover, in the seventeenth century, there grew up institutions whose practical achievement, if not ostensible purpose, was to eliminate the unwanted children of the poor: both foundling hospitals and workhouses were highly effective infanticide agencies. In early eighteenth-century London, the latter were killing off some 88 percent of their children, and indeed in some parishes it was reported that "no infant had lived to be apprenticed from their workhouses."[64]

As a result of all these factors, fertility among the upper classes was very high indeed, and the peers had an effective generation replacement rate of unparalleled magnitude—as high as 1.5 for those born between 1550 and 1600. In other words between about 1580 and 1630 the children of peers were producing 50 percent more children per generation.[65] The intense competition for jobs and offices in the decades before the Civil War can best be understood in the light of this remarkable demographic phenomenon.

(3) PRICE REVOLUTION. Largely, but not entirely, as a result of this demographic growth, prices rose by between 400 percent and 650 percent from 1500 to 1640. Food prices (and therefore agricultural profits) soared, wages and other less adaptable revenues lagged behind. Whole social and occupational groups rose or fell as a result.

(4) FREE LAND MARKET. Between 1534 and 1650 the Crown seized all the revenues of the monasteries and the chantries, and substantial portions of those of the bishops. To pay for war, it immediately sold much of it, the rest being disposed of at intervals under financial stress. Including all sales of Crown and Church

lands, as much as 25 percent to 30 percent of the total landed area of the country, which had previously been locked up in institutional hands, may have been released on to the private market between 1534 and 1660. By the Restoration the process was virtually complete.[66]

This throwing of Crown and Church lands on to the market was accompanied by an equally important development which released a huge mass of private property which had previously been tied up by legal restrictions against alienation. In the late Middle Ages the entail was a fairly effective barrier against the free disposition of ' property by the current owner; in the late seventeenth century the strict settlement served the same purpose. Between 1530 and 1660, however, there were relatively few and weak legal obstacles to the alienation of property. The result of this legal situation and of various economic pressures was the massive transfer of land by purchase and sale, which reached a peak in the 1610s. It should be noted that both factors involved, the seizure and dispersal of Church lands and the freeing of private property from restrictions on alienation, were the result of politico-legal action supported and encouraged by the landed classes themselves.

(5) INCREASED COMMERICAL ACTIVITY.   Foreign trade expanded in sudden bursts, particularly from 1508 to 1551, 1603 to 1620, and 1660 to 1688. More important, but less easy to document, may have been the growth of credit and transport facilities, and the consequent expansion of market activity inside the country. Their development increased both the numbers and the amount and range of mobility of the merchants.

(6) INCREASED LITIGATION.   The end of violence, the growth of commercial activity, and the opening of the land market enormously increased the volume of litigation, the main result of which was to transfer wealth from the landed classes to the lawyers.[67]

(7) THE PURITAN ETHIC.   The Puritans took a strongly moralistic—indeed medieval—approach to economic affairs, and the Puritan merchant was consequently subject to almost intolerable psychological pressures as he strove both to maximize profits and to conform to ethical doctrines of the just price.[68] On the other hand, insistent Puritan indoctrination on self-discipline and the virtue of striving in the calling could hardly avoid producing personalities

with strong anal-erotic characteristics and a high achievement motive. Once the children were grown up, their obsession with thrift and hard, rationally planned work carried them inexorably along towards the corruptions of wealth and upward social mobility.

There is some reason to believe, however, that this ideological factor did not become fully operative until the 1630s, for its best theoretical expression comes from Richard Baxter. Moreover, evidence of close association of religious Dissent with commercial success does not become plentiful until after the Restoration. Even then the association may have been as much an incidental by-product of exclusion from social and political life under the Clarendon Code as a direct consequence of religious ideology.

More important than this possible economic link are the indirect and accidental consequences of Puritanism. One is the stress the Puritans laid on Bible-reading, and hence the spread of elementary education. Another is the self-confidence and sense of righteousness arising from contract theology and the doctrine of the Elect, which gave men the assurance to aspire high and to challenge their social, economic, and political superiors. Furthermore the democratic, or at the very least oligarchic, tendencies of Puritan church organization worked against the heirarchical and authoritarian concept of society and was thus a destabilizing force. "Purity is Parity" was the slogan of their Anglican enemies, and there was something in the taunt.

Finally one can point to certain chronological correspondences which are, at the very least, suggestive of interconnections. The great age of social mobility precisely coincides with the great age of Puritanism. It is also, perhaps, rather too much of a coincidence that a content anaylsis of popular literature reveals a high peak of achievement motifs at precisely the same period.[69] This period of widespread challenges to the official system of values contrasts sharply with the post-Restoration development of Divine Right and Passive Obedience notions, and still more with the smug complacency with which Englishmen regarded the existing social and political order after the Glorious Revolution of 1688.

(8) EDUCATIONAL EXPANSION.   The period 1560 to 1640 saw an unprecedented educational boom, which affected all but the lowest

levels of society. This did not only produce quantitatively a remarkably literate society; it also turned out an educated gentry and aristocracy in excess of the capacity of government service to absorb them, and lower-class clergymen in excess of the cures of souls available. If for many the fruits of this educational expansion were bitter, the spread of literacy and the increased opportunities for higher education for the children of yeomen and artisans must have increased the possibility of upward mobility for intellectual talent.[70] The secularization of the state may have destroyed the opportunity for the occasional child of the moderately humble to shoot up via the church to high political office, but the growth of education and of the professions opened up other and wider avenues to hardly less exalted positions.

After 1640 first the disturbance of the Civil War and then the social reaction of the Restoration put an end to the expansion of secondary and higher education, which went into a decline. After 1660 opportunities for social advancement via the professions must have been proportionately reduced, and confined to those who could still gain access to this narrowed educational ladder.

(9) REVOLUTIONARY POLITICAL ACTION. One would have supposed that the political upheavals of the English Revolution between 1640 and 1660 must have produced far-reaching social changes. Now it is certainly true that revolutionary activity was itself a vehicle for social mobility, in that previously submerged individuals, low-born parsons like Stephen Marshall, backwoods gentry like Oliver Cromwell, frustrated petty bourgeois like John Lilburne, found an opportunity to take the centre of the stage and even to seize power from their social superiors.

But the temporary collapse of the traditional order and the temporary inversion of roles had no lasting effect upon English society. It has been shown conclusively that the old landlords, even the Royalists, survived the Interregnum far better than might have been expected. No new class of successful generals, entrepreneurs, and Parliamentary committee men arose out of the 1650s, if only because Church, Crown, and Royalist lands were nearly all restored to their former owners at the Restoration.[71] Lower down the social scale the schemes of the Levellers for converting copyhold tenure into freehold were defeated, and the tenantry and small

freeholders were probably depressed by the burden of war taxation, plunder, and billeting, rather than elevated by any new official
concern for their welfare. The rising government debt and the
expansion of government services enhanced the prestige and
increased the fortunes of financiers, contractors, and leading
officials, but the significance of these factors does not seem to have
been very great. Society in 1660 looked much as it had in 1640, and
the number of new families who had risen, or old families who had
fallen, over the previous twenty years does not seem to have been at
all exceptional. In terms of permanent social change (as opposed to
a permanent legacy of ideas) the English Revolution was the least
successful of all the "Great Revolutions" in history.

Stabilizing Factors, 1650–1700

During the course of the late seventeenth century, a series of
stabilizing factors became operative which severely dampened the
process of social mobility, and at the same time eased social
tensions.

(1) Of the main destabilizing factors, demographic growth, price
revolution, free land market, educational expansion, Puritan ideological enthusiasm, and revolutionary activity had all been substantially reduced by 1660, some of them beginning to decline as early
as 1620.

(2) There was a sharp drop in fertility and a sharp rise in
mortality among the upper classes, so that cohorts born between
1625 and 1674 were barely reproducing themselves, and those
between 1675 and 1749 were actually falling behind.[72] This dramatic change from the pre-Civil War condition of an excess of
children to be accommodated in a relatively static job market must
enormously have reduced social competition twenty-five years
later, that is after 1660.

(3) The natural result of a long period of social mobility, followed
by civil war and violent political and social upheaval, was a
determination in the minds of all classes to put a damper on
change, and to reassert traditional control by traditional authorities.[73] Although in some respects it only accelerated trends already
visible in Early Stuart society, this post-Restoration conservative

reaction was perhaps the most striking practical consequence of the Revolution. The results can be seen most clearly in the field of education, which was now carefully adjusted to the needs of the élite. Between 1570 and 1650 secondary and university education had been running wild, resulting in a free-for-all competitive struggle uncontrolled by the existing élite, which produced a surplus of qualified men for the available élite jobs, and which failed to indoctrinate them with élite values and élite behaviour patterns. Hence the lamentations of conservatives like Bacon and Hobbes in the early seventeenth century that education was undermining the basis of established society. After the Restoration, however, educational opportunities at this higher level were sharply reduced, and English educational patterns settled down to that tradition of "sponsored mobility" which it has retained ever since. By this system a minority of youths are selected by the élite and their agents at an early age for training in classical studies and aesthetic appreciation, in preparation for admission into this exclusive world. The eighteenth-century grammar schools and universities with their limited scholarship facilities, and the public schools of the nineteenth century, both performed this task of indoctrinating the aspiring few with the ideals and values of the existing élite. A recurrence of the dangerously competitive situation of the early seventeenth century has consequently been avoided ever since.

This adjustment of the educational system was only achieved, however, at considerable intellectual cost. It was not only in terms of quantity that English education declined: qualitatively, the Ancients triumphed over the Moderns, and enforced their view of the role of classical studies in the curriculum; socially the Royal Society, after a promising beginning as an intellectual group open to talent regardless of rank, degenerated into a club for gentlemanly dilettantes.[74] By 1720 England had lost its scientific pre-eminence, and the universities had sunk into a torpor which only the pen of Gibbon could adequately describe.

Parallel to this development, rule by a narrow élite was strengthened at all levels of government. Control of the parish fell into the hands of select vestries of "the better sort." County administration, for example in Northamptonshire, was confined to a smaller, more stable, and more closed-off élite group of families.[75] In the towns the same process had long been at work as control of both guilds and civic government passed into the hands of an ever smaller and less fluid oligarchy. At the Freeman level the same thing was happening, and at York the closing of the ranks seems to have occurred before the end of the sixteenth century. In 1509–18, only 16 percent of Freemen were sons of Freemen, but the proportion had jumped to 38 percent by 1594–1603, and to 43 percent by 1675–99. The same trend is visible at Leicester, and its continuance is indicated by the rise of patrimony and purchase as means of entry into several of the Livery Companies of London in the eighteenth century.[76]

In both the Church and government service, hereditary succession became more marked. In the former this was an inevitable by-product of clerical marriage and growing respect for the dignity of the cloth. In the dioceses of Oxford and Worcester, the proportion of parish clergy who were the sons of clergymen rose from 5 percent in 1600 to 23 percent in 1640. In the 1630s, over a quarter of the bishops were sons of clergymen.[77] By 1660 the Anglican Church was well on the way to becoming a markedly hereditary profession.

Well before the Civil War there is evidence of considerable nepotism in government service. In the early seventeenth century, patrimony and patronage were the two principal keys to entry into government service, with purchase a bad third. The role of patrimony is shown by the fact that the fathers of more than half the officials who were sons of peers or knights had themselves been in government service. Of the whole body, 18 percent were second generation in royal service. Almost half came from the squirearchy and above, and about two thirds from the gentry or above. The critical question is whether or not the situation was getting worse, and this we just do not know. Charles I was certainly reacting against this tendency in the 1630s, but this may be evidence of a new political attitude towards the bureaucracy by the absolute monarch rather than of any actual change in recruitment patterns.[78] All one can say is that an increasing trend towards nepotism and social exclusiveness is what *a priori* one would expect to result from the very high reproduction rate of the landed classes over the previous sixty years.

V CONSEQUENCES

The Century of Mobility, 1540–1640

Modern societies are learning slowly that widening opportunities and rapid mobility are not necessarily conducive to human contentment. Given the traditional and conservative value system of the age, the great increase in mobility of all kinds in the hundred years from 1540 to 1640 probably created discontent rather than satisfaction, due primarily to the wide discrepancies which developed between the three sectors of wealth, status, and power.

(1) SOCIAL DISCONTENT. This was felt by both the upwardly and downwardly mobile. One economically rising group, the merchants, felt themselves denied social prestige, and resented the affront. Other economically advancing groups, the successful lawyers and the greater squires, felt themselves excluded from power by the Court, and also resented the affront. Of the declining groups, the wage-earners were in a state of abject misery which found intermittent relief in rioting and mob violence. The clergy lamented their loss of income and status relative to those of the laity, and under Laud they allied themselves with the Crown in a vain attempt to recover both. An economically static group, the humble parish gentry, resented their stagnation and were consumed with envy at the conspicuous success of merchants, courtiers, and squires. Those nearest London felt the resentment most keenly, since they were most aware of the discrepancy in opportunities. Though the gentry of the home counties were better off economically than those of the north and west they were more bitter since they knew what they were missing. Hence the loyalty to Church and King of the poor backwoodsmen of the west and north in the Civil War, and the rallying to the Independent cause of a section of the small gentry of the home counties.

(2) RELIGIOUS DISCONTENT. How Puritanism affected mobility has already been discussed, but we must now examine how mobility affected Puritanism. After all, the two rose and fell together in extraordinary unison, and a reciprocal feed-back system of causation is by no means theoretically impossible. Professor Walzer has suggested that rigid self-discipline at the service of an ideology is one possible response to a condition of anxiety induced by the

overthrow of stable social relationships and agreed political, ethical, and religious ideals; cheerful opportunism, quietistic withdrawal, and fierce nostalgia for a lost world are others.[79] It is not difficult to understand the predicament of the late sixteenth- and early seventeenth-century Englishmen as the ancient props of their universe fell away. Competing religious ideologies shattered the unquestioning and habit-forming faith of the past; the failure of the Anglican Church to put its house in order left it open to every enterprising undergraduate to draw up an alternative scheme for ecclesiastical organization; constitutional conflicts between Commons and Crown disturbed conventional notions of the role of the state and posed the insoluble question of sovereignty; the collapse of the quasi-feudal ties of hereditary dependence left men free to seek clientage where they could find it; the decline of the craft guilds freed labour from both rules and companionship; the bonds of kinship were loosened under pressure from new religious and political associations, and from new ideals of love and freedom within the nuclear family. The upsetting of the hierarchy of status as a result of rapid social mobility was thus just one of many factors which generated unease, anxiety, anomie.

At present, it is hardly possible to identify Puritanism as the ideology of groups clearly moving in any particular direction. Many were undoubtedly members of upwardly mobile groups seeking security, companionship, and assured status in the emerging society of the seventeenth century. There were newly risen Henrician peers and officials like the Dudleys, Cecils, Norths; rich squires at last freed from dependence on aristocratic power, like Knightley, Barrington, and Hampden; new academics and preaching ministers like Laurence Chaderton and Anthony Gilby; new merchants, shopkeepers, and artisans in the flourishing towns. Others were members of the static small gentry class bewildered by the transformation around them and seeking some support, like Oliver Cromwell. Both revolutionary Puritanism and the reactionary "Church and King" conservatism of Laud, Strafford, and the backwoods Royalists are alternate responses to identical pressures of social change. On the other hand, many of the key figures in the movement, like their Huguenot counterparts in France, seem to belong to rich, ancient, self-confident families, who should have been immune from such fears. The thesis is an attractive one, but there are still many loose ends to be tidied up.

The Decades of Revolution, 1640–60

I have argued at length elsewhere that it was the temporary decline in status and income of the nobles relative to the gentry which allowed the House of Commons to take the centre of the political stage; and that it was this decline in prestige, together with a similar decline of the higher clergy and the ineptitude of the remedies adopted by the Stuarts, which allowed the gentry in the Commons successfully to challenge the establishment in Church and State in 1640. Furthermore it was their vision of an increasingly corrupt, wealthy, wasteful, and wicked Establishment which galvanized the squirearchy into action. Finally, it was the rise in education and in numbers of the urban petty bourgeois, especially of London, which made possible the development of the Leveller Party and of Leveller ideas in the late 1640s. If these hypotheses are correct, the shifts in wealth and prestige among the various status and occupational groups, and the "contest mobility" created by the expansion of education during the previous hundred years, played no small part in generating the tensions that led to political breakdown in 1640, to Civil War in 1642, and to the emergence of radicalism in 1647.

Post-Restoration Stability, 1660–1700

One of the obvious conclusions of this paper is that much more, and more sociologically and statistically sophisticated, research is needed before we will be in a position to confirm or refute some of the most basic assumptions that are commonly made about the character of early modern English society. Contemporaries asserted, and posterity has followed them in believing, that by European standards England was an exceptionally mobile society in the sixteenth, seventeenth, and eighteenth centuries, and that this was perhaps the main reason why England was the first European nation to industrialize and why it was successful in avoiding bloody revolution in the process. Now there is no doubt that primogeniture and the confining of a title to the eldest son ensured a steady flow of downwardly mobile younger sons, and so made English society at all times different from that of Europe. But recent work on France has revealed a hitherto unsuspected degree of upward mobility in the apparently caste-structured society of the *ancien régime*. It was Turgot who remarked that *"il n'est aucun homme riche qui sur le champ ne devienne noble; en sorte que le corps de nobles comprend tout le corps des riches."*[80] It may well be that it was only in the century 1540–1640, when land was changing hands at a speed which was quite unprecedented between 1200 and 1900, that there was any unusual mobility in the upper ranks of English society as a whole. Could it be that English society closed ranks a century earlier than France, in the late seventeenth instead of the late eighteenth century, and that the reputation enjoyed by pre-industrial England as an unusually mobile society is largely an illusion based on false assumptions and a dearth of statistical evidence?

If high mobility was only a temporary phenomenon, however, it effected certain structural changes which had profound and lasting results, and which undoubtedly made England rather different from France in the age of Voltaire. The first was the increase in numbers of the squirearchy and gentry, which had far-reaching political and social consequences. Politically, it meant a massive numerical extension of the political nation and so provided the basis for the eighteenth-century constitutional system, which was operated in rough conformity to the interests and aspirations of this broad-based class.

Socially, it meant that for the first time in history the majority of the population were living directly under the eye of a member of the ruling élite. If we may generalize from Buckinghamshire and Rutlandshire, in 1522 only about one village in ten had a resident squire; by 1680 the proportion in the whole country had risen to over two thirds.[81] The potentialities for social and political control were thus greatly increased over what they had been two hundred years before.

The second structural change was the rise of the commercial and professional classes in numbers and wealth, and their consequent acquisition both of a share in political decision-making and of social recognition. The massive increase in numbers had the important social function of absorbing the younger sons pushed out of the landed classes by the primogeniture system. The merchants had little formal power but their economic interests closely interlocked with those of the landed classes, thanks to the dependence of the price of land on the price of wool, in turn dependent on the cloth export trade. The maintenance of this trade was also of vital concern to the government, since a slump not only created a threat to social stability in the clothing areas due to unemployment, but also reduced government revenue from the customs. Furthermore, the growing role of the leading London merchants as government creditors and contractors, culminating in the foundation of the Bank of England, gave them considerable behind-the-scenes influence. As a result, foreign, military, and economic policies were increasingly conducted with an eye to the interests, and with the advice, of this merchant élite.[82]

Along with their admission to the political nation went a rise in their social status. There was a slow but steady shift of attitudes on the part of the landed classes, a growing recognition that the previously anomalous occupational categories formed a series of semi-independent and parallel status hierarchies—the "San Gimignano model." By the late seventeenth century merchants, lawyers, clergymen, and officials were held in much less contempt than they had been a century earlier. The hypothesis (which has yet to be proved) that many of these middle-class occupational groups were of gentry origin would make it that much easier for the landed classes to treat them with respect. It was perhaps this which gave foreigners the illusion that England was a more mobile society than their own.

Three consequences followed from this rise in status. Firstly, there was much more intermarriage between the landed classes and the appropriate economic strata of these occupational groups. Thus of the 105 armigerous gentry of Warwickshire recognized by the Heralds in 1682, two thirds had mercantile connections (mostly with London) built into their pedigrees somewhere, though only a handful may have owed their economic prosperity primarily to this source. Secondly, the gentry lost their earlier reluctance to put their sons into trade. By the middle third of the seventeenth century nearly half the Freemen of the Drapers' Company of

Shrewsbury and nearly a fifth of the London Stationers' Company apprentices were coming from gentry stock.[83] Thirdly, the business or professional man could acquire the title of "Gent.," and on occasion even "Esq.," without having to buy an estate and cut himself off from his economic roots. As early as 1635, there were nearly 1,200 persons resident in London who described themselves as gentlemen, the great majority of whom were engaged in trade or in some professional occupation. In one Hundred of Warwickshire, in the late seventeenth century, a third of the "gentlemen" of the area were now resident in the town of Warwick, and most of them were probably earning their living there.[84] The substantial shrinkage of land offered for sale on the market thus coincided with a distinct, if less pronounced, shrinkage of demand. An estate was still essential for entry into the restricted élite who wielded political and administrative power at both county and national levels, but it was no longer necessary in order to be recognized as the social equal of a minor landed gentleman. If 1540–1640 saw the rise of the gentry, 1600–1700 saw the rise of the "pseudo-gentry."

A striking example of this development is Henry Bell. He was born in 1647, his father being an alderman of King's Lynn, a mercer by trade, and twice mayor of the town. Henry was educated at the local grammar-school and at Cambridge, then spent his life as a merchant and civic dignitary of Lynn, following in his father's footsteps as alderman and twice mayor of the town. But despite this impeccably bourgeois family career, Bell had gone on the Grand Tour, and was a virtuoso whose great passion in life seems to have been the arts. He wrote a treatise on the invention of painting before the Flood, he was one of the half-dozen Englishmen with a good professional knowledge of Italian architecture, and he practiced as an architect on the side. On the other hand his clientele was as urban as himself, being the corporation of Northampton, who enlisted his services in the rebuilding of the town after a disastrous fire, and the authorities and dignitaries of his home town of Lynn.[85] Here in the flesh is the true *bourgeois gentilhomme,* the self-assured townsman and tradesman with the education, the values, and the interests of the cultivated aristocrat. He is a peculiarly English phenomenon, impossible before the late seventeenth century, whose like was unknown to Molière.

Further evidence of this trend rather further down the social scale may be seen in the blurring of that previously crucial division between gentlemen and others by the emergence of a new titular group, sandwiched in between, and comprising parts of the lesser gentry on the one hand and the upper yeomanry and shopkeepers on the other. These were the people, the numbers of whom were steadily increasing as the seventeenth century wore on, whose names in official lists, etc., were prefixed by the word "Mr."[86] By 1700 the topmost elements of Group 3 and the lowest elements of Group 4 were beginning to form another status group of their own.

These two structural changes caused by the mobility of the previous hundred years were accompanied in the late seventeenth century by that deliberate restriction of mobility channels which has already been described. At the upper levels there was the narrowing of the avenues of mobility, partly by legal changes devised to preserve existing fortunes and property, and to restrict to established families access to positions of wealth and power; partly by biological changes which caused the striking reduction of the reproduction rate of the upper classes between 1630 and 1740; and partly by economic changes which shut off the disturbing forces of demographic growth and price inflation. At the lower level there was the attempted restriction of horizontal mobility by the pass-law system introduced by the Act of Settlement of 1662; the reduction of educational opportunities to a pattern of carefully sponsored mobility for a selected few; the reduction of the last remaining democratic elements in parish, guild, and urban government; and the perversion of the national electoral process by the extravagant use of corruption. These developments prepared the way for the political and social stability of the century following the Glorious Revolution of 1688, during which England was governed by a broad-based but relatively closed oligarchy, part landed, part monied, under the leadership of a still narrower élite of extremely wealthy and influential noble landowners.

CHAPTER 1

1. L. Stone, *The Crisis of the Aristocracy, 1558–1641* (Oxford, 1965), pp. 49–53, is an earlier attempt to tackle this problem. The present analysis provides what is hoped to be a more sophisticated model.

2. A. J. and R. H. Tawney, "An Occupational Census of the Seventeenth Century," *Econ. Hist. Rev.*, v (1934–5), p. 47. P. Laslett, "Clayworth and Cogenhoe," in *Historical Essays, 1600–1750*, ed. H. E. Bell and R. L. Ollard (London, 1963), p. 169; and data extracted from "Lay Subsidy Rolls, 1524–25," *Sussex Record Society*, lvi (1957).

3. L. Stone, *op. cit.*, p. 40. W. G. Hoskins, "The Elizabethan Merchants of Exeter," in *Elizabethan Government and Society*, ed. S. T. Bindoff *et al.* (London, 1961), pp. 166–70, 176, 185–6. W. T. MacCaffrey, *Exeter, 1540–1640* (Cambridge, Mass., 1958), pp. 260–4. P. McGrath, "Records relating to the Society of Merchant Adventurers of the City of Bristol in the Seventeenth Century," *Bristol Rec. Soc.*, xvii (1953), pp. xxviii–xxx. *V.C.H., Yorks., The City of York* (London, 1961), pp. 180–1. T. S. Willan, *The Muscovy Merchants of 1555* (Manchester, 1953), pp. 69–74. Willan casts some doubts on the truth of this picture, but he offers no hard statistical evidence to back up his suspicions.

4. L. Stone, "The Educational Revolution in England, 1560–1640," *Past and Present*, no. 28 (July, 1964), pp. 58–9. R. Robson, *The Attorney in Eighteenth Century England* (Cambridge, 1959).

5. D. M. Barratt, "The Condition of the Parish Clergy between the Reformation and 1660" (Oxford D.Phil. thesis, 1949), pp. 18, 180–206. F. W. Brooks, "The Social Position of the Parson in the Sixteenth Century," *Brit. Arch. Ass. Jl.*, 3rd ser., x (1948). W. G. Hoskins, "The Leicestershire Country Parson in the Sixteenth Century," in his *Essays in Leicestershire History* (Liverpool, 1950), pp. 1–23.

6. Stone, *Crisis*, pp. 40, 405–11. This social pattern (the information about which I owe to Mr. F. S. Odo, a member of my research seminar at Princeton) hardly differs from that of the pre-Reformation church of the 1520s and thirties.

7. G. E. Aylmer, *The King's Servants* (London, 1961), p. 263.

8. Gregory King's figures suggest that in 1690 only about 15 percent of the population was living in towns of more than 1,000 (two-thirds of whom were

crowded into London). D. V. Glass, "Two papers on Gregory King," in D. V. Glass and D. E. C. Eversley, *Population in History* (London, 1965), pp. 174, 178.

9. S.M. Lipset and R. Bendix, *Social Mobility in Industrial Society* (Berkeley, 1959), p. 27.

10. For this distinction see Ralph H. Turner, "Sponsored and Contest Mobility and the School System," *Amer. Soc. Rev.*, xxv (1960), pp. 855–67.

11. T. Wilson, "The State of England Anno Dom. 1600," *Camden Misc.*, xvi (1936). C. B. Macpherson, *The Political Theory of Possessive Individualism* (Oxford, 1962), pp. 280–1.

12. MacCaffrey, *op. cit.*, pp. 16–17, 22–5, 251–6. Hoskins, "Elizabethan Merchants of Exeter," *loc. cit.*, pp. 163–6. J. E. Neale, *The Elizabethan House of Commons* (London, 1949), *passim*.

13. D. C. Coleman, "Labour in the English Economy in the Seventeenth Century," *Econ. Hist. Rev.*, 2nd ser., viii (1955–6), pp. 280–95. W. G. Hoskins, *Provincial England* (London, 1963), p. 83. J. Cornwall, "The People of Rutland in 1522," *Leics. Arch. Soc. Trans.*, xxxvii (1961–2), p. 15; "English Country Towns in the 1520s," *Econ. Hist. Rev.*, 2nd ser., xv (1962–3), p. 66. Macpherson, *op. cit.*, pp. 280–1. W. G. Hoskins, *The Midland Peasant* (London, 1957), p. 195. C. H. Wilson, *England's Apprenticeship 1600–1763* (London, 1965), pp. 231–6, 343–7. W. G. Hoskins, *Industry, Trade and People in Exeter, 1688–1800* (Manchester, 1935), pp. 115–6.

14. A. G. Dickens, *The English Reformation* (London, 1964), pp. 163–6. Stone, *Crisis*, ch. iii. J. Cornwall, "The Early Tudor Gentry," *Econ. Hist. Rev.*, 2nd ser., xvii (1964–5), pp. 457–61. Macpherson, *op. cit.*, pp. 280–1.

15. W. R. Prest, "Some Aspects of the Inns of Court 1590–1640" (Oxford D.Phil. thesis, 1965), p. 385. E. Foss, *Lives of the Judges* (London, 1857), v, pp. 107–8, 421–4; vi, pp. 35–7, 234–6. *H. M. C. Rutland MSS.*, iv. p. 216. *Cal. State Papers Dom., 1633–4*, p. 251. J. Aubrey, *The Natural History of Wiltshire*, ed. J. Britton (London, 1847), part ii, ch. xvi. Macpherson, *op. cit.*, p. 180.

16. J. H. Raach, *A Directory of English Country Physicians, 1603–43* (London, 1962). R. S. Roberts, "The Personnel and Practice of Medicine in Tudor and Stuart England," *Medical History*, vi (1962); viii (1964).

17. W. T. MacCaffrey, "Place and Patronage in Elizabethan Politics," in *Elizabethan Government and Society*, ed. S. T. Bindoff *et al.* (London, 1961), ·pp. 106–8. Aylmer, *op. cit.*, p. 254; and "Place Bills and the Separation of Powers," *Trans. Roy. Hist. Soc.*, 5th ser., xv (1965), pp. 65–6. These very rough guesses for 1690 I owe to the kindness of Professor Daniel Baugh. The firm figures for central office-holders in the late eighteenth century are derived from *The Report of the Commissioners on Fees, 1786–7* (P. P., 1806, vol. vii). *Reports of Committees*, vol. xi, pp. 114 ff., 200 ff. *Commons Journals*, vol. xli, pp. 9 ff.; vol. xlii, pp. 48 ff.

18. Stone, *op. cit.*, pp. 274–94. Wilson, *op. cit.*, p. 17. Examples of the new kind of secretarial/professional careers in private and royal service are those of Edward Palavicino at a lower level and John Pym and Sir Benjamin Rudyard at a higher: L. Stone, *An Elizabethan: Sir Horatio Palavicino* (Oxford, 1956), pp. 316–20; M. F. Keeler, *The Long Parliament, 1640–41* (Philadelphia, 1954), pp. 318–9, 329.

19. E. H. Phelps Brown and S. V. Hopkins, "Seven Centuries of Prices of Consumables compared with Builders' Wage-rates," *Economica*, xxiii (1956), repr. in *Essays in Economic History*, vol. ii, ed. E. M. Carus-Wilson (London, 1962)

20. W. Harrison, *Description of England*, in R. H. Tawney and E. Power, *Tudor Economic Documents* (London, 1924), iii, pp. 68–72. R. Reyce, *The Breviary of Suffolk*, ed. Francis Lord Hervey (London, 1902), pp. 49–52. F. Bacon, "Observations on a Libel," in J. Spedding, *Life and Letters of Sir Francis Bacon* (London, 1890), i, pp. 158–9. W. G. Hoskins, ed., *Essays in Leicestershire History* (Liverpool, 1950), pp. 132–6, 179–83; "Elizabethan Merchants of Exeter," *loc. cit.*, pp. 178–83. M. W. Barley, *The English Farmhouse and Cottage* (London, 1961), pp. 38–179. W. G. Hoskins, "The Rebuilding of Rural England, 1570–1640," *Past and Present*, no. 4 (Nov., 1953); *The Midland Peasant* (London, 1957), pp. 185–6, 296–8.

21. This observation is based on a survey of the evidence in the counties covered so far by N. Pevsner in the Penguin *Building of England* series.

22. For the wealth of the Jacobean aldermen, see R. G. Lang, "The Greater Merchants of London in the early Seventeenth Century" (Oxford D.Phil. thesis, 1963). Some figures for officially recorded personal incomes are given in W. K. Jordan, *The Charities of London, 1480–1660* (London, 1960), pp. 53–4.

23. Stone, *Crisis*, pp. 156–64, 470–6.

24. C. Hill, *Economic Problems of the Church* (Oxford, 1956), ch. ix.

25. *The Journal of James Yonge*, ed. F. N. L. Poynter (London, 1963).

26. H. J. Habakkuk, "English Landownership, 1680–1740," *Econ. Hist. Rev.*, x (1940); "La Disparition du Paysan Anglais," *Annales E.S.C.*, xx (1965).

27. See above, note 5.

28. R. Robson, *op. cit.*, ch. iii.

29. Stone, *op. cit.*, pp. 119–22, 163–4, 266–70, 476–81, 662–8, 743–53.

30. P. Zagorin, "The Court and the Country," *Eng. Hist. Rev.*, lxxvii (1962), pp. 306–11. Aylmer, "Place-bills," *loc. cit.*

31. Stone, *op. cit.*, ch. v. M. E. James, *Change and Continuity in the Tudor North* (Borthwick Papers, xxvii, York, 1965).

32. Macpherson, *op. cit.*, p. 280. Professor Baugh tells me that he thinks King substantially overestimated the number of officials in the upper category.

33. E. E. Rich, "The Population of Elizabethan England," *Econ. Hist. Rev.*, 2nd ser., ii (1949–50), p. 259. P. Styles, "A Census of a Warwickshire Village in 1698," *Univ. of Birmingham Hist. Jl.*, iii (1951), pp. 45–8. Laslett, "Clayworth and Cogenhoe," *loc. cit.*, p. 183. L. M. Marshall, "The Rural Population of Bedfordshire, 1671 to 1921," *Beds. Hist. Rec. Soc.*, xvi (1934), pp. 53–64.

34. G. H. Tupling, *The Economic History of Rossendale* (Manchester, 1927), pp. 42–97. J. Thirsk, *Fenland Farming in the Sixteenth Century* (Leicester, 1953), pp. 21–2. M. Campbell, *The English Yeoman* (New Haven, 1942), pp. 72, 93–7. P. A. J. Pettit, "Charles I and the Revival of Forest Law in Northamptonshire," *Northamptonshire Past and Present*, iii (1961), p. 54. E. Kerridge, "The Revolts in Wiltshire against Charles I," *Wilts. Arch. Magazine*, lvii (1958), pp. 66–70.

35.

Date	London	England and Wales	Percent
1500	60,000	3,000,000	2
1600	225,000	4,500,000	5
1700	550,000	5,500,000	10

C. Creighton, "The Population of Old London," *Blackwood's Magazine*, cxlix (Edinburgh, Apr., 1891). N. G. Brett-James, *The Growth of Stuart London* (London,

1935), ch. xx. Wilson, *op. cit.,* p. 47. W. G. Hoskins, *Provincial England* (London, 1963), ch. iv. MacCaffrey, *Exeter,* pp. 12–13.

36. *The Writings of John Greenwood, 1587–90,* ed. L. H. Carlson (London, 1962), p. 198.

37. P. Styles, "The Social Structure of Kineton Hundred in the Reign of Charles II," *Birmingham Arch. Soc. Trans.,* lxxviii (1962), p. 100.

38. S. L. Thrupp, *The Merchant Class of Medieval London* (Chicago, 1948), p. 211. C. Welch, *Register of Freeman of the City of London in the Reigns of Henry VIII and Edward VI* (London, 1908). Kahl, *op. cit.,* pp. 17–20. C. Blagden, "The Stationers' Company in the Eighteenth Century," *Guildhall Miscellany,* x (1959), pp. 36–52. Bower Marsh, *Records of the Worshipful Company of Carpenters* (Oxford, 1913–39), vols. i and vi. Guildhall Library, MSS. 5576/1–3 (Fishmongers); 5184/1 (Bakers). For a discussion of the changing social and economic role of apprenticeship and freedom of a Company, see J. F. Kellett, "The Breakdown of Gild and Corporation Control over the Handicraft and Retail Trade of London," *Econ. Hist. Rev.,* 2nd ser., x (1957–8). E. J. Buckatsch, "Place of Origin of a Group of Immigrants into Sheffield, 1624–1799," *Econ. Hist. Rev.,* 2nd ser., ii (1949–50), p. 305.

39. *Cambridge History of the British Empire* (Cambridge, 1929), i, p. 179. S. C. Powell, *Puritan Village* (Middlebury, Conn., 1963), pp. 18–29, 92–116. M. Campbell, *op. cit.,* pp. 279–80.

40. I owe this point to Dr. Kenneth Lockridge.

41. T. O. Ranger, "Richard Boyle and the making of an Irish fortune, 1588–1614," *Irish Historical Studies,* x (1957). A. B. Grosart, *The Lismore Papers, 1886–88,* 2nd ser., iv, p. 259. Brit. Mus., Harleian MSS., 991, p. 8.

42. Stone, *op. cit.,* p. 37, fig. I. That this rise and fall is a solid reality is supported by a study of the mobility of manorial property in Surrey between 1840 and 1700, carried out by Mr. F. M. Brodhead, a member of my research seminar at Princeton. He has shown that the market for this sort of property was all but dead before the dissolution of the monasteries, and that it was this political act which set the process in motion; he has also confirmed that the movement reached its peak in the early seventeenth century and then died away again.

43. M. Curtis, "The Alienated Intellectuals of Early Stuart England," *Past and Present,* no. 23 (Nov., 1962). Hill, *op. cit.,* ch. ix.

44. Campbell, *op. cit.,* ch. v.

45. MacCaffrey, *Exeter,* pp. 269–70. W. G. Hoskins, *Essays in Leichestershire History* (Liverpool, 1955), ch. iv., and "An Elizabethan Provincial Town: Leicester," in his *Provincial England,* p. 107. Stone, *Crisis,* pp. 285–94.

46. *Op. cit.,* p. 190. J. T. Cliffe, "The Yorkshire Gentry on the Eve of the Civil War" (London Ph.D. thesis, 1960), p. 96.

47. H. J. Habakkuk, "The English Land Market in the Eighteenth Century," in J. S. Bromley and E. H. Kossmann, eds., *Britain and the Netherlands,* ii (London, 1959), pp. 168–73.

48. Stone, *op. cit.,* pp. 191–94.

49. L. B. Namier and J. Brooke, *The House of Commons, 1754–1790* (London, 1964), p. 104.

50. R. H. Tawney, "The Rise of the Gentry, 1558–1640," *Econ. Hist. Rev.,* xi (1941), repr. in *Essays in Economic History,* vol. i, ed. E. M. Carus-Wilson (London, 1954), pp. 173–4, 192.

51. Stone, *op. cit.,* pp. 629–32.

52. J. Le Goff and R. Romano, "Paysages et Peuplement rural en Europe après le XIe Siècle," Comité International des Sciences Historiques, XIIe Congrès International, 1965, *Rapports,* iii, pp. 21–2.

53. Stone, *op. cit.,* pp. 178–83.

54. *Op. cit.,* App. xxx. T. H. Hollingsworth, *The Demography of the British Peerage,* Supplement to *Population Studies,* xviii (1965), p. 9. H. Tilly, *The Vendée* (Cambridge, Mass.), 1964, p. 97.

55. R. G. Lang, "The Greater Merchants of London in the early Seventeenth Century" (Oxford D.Phil. thesis, 1963). Hoskins, "The Elizabethan Merchants of Exeter," *loc. cit.,* p. 167.

56. Stone, *op. cit.,* pp. 21–36.

57. *Op. cit.,* pp. 184–88, 547–86.

58. *V. C. H., Leics.,* (London, 1955) iii, pp. 137–47. W. G. Hoskins, "The Population of an English Village, 1086–1801: a study of Wigston Magna," in his *Provincial England,* pp. 185–200. Lionel Munby, *Hertfordshire Population Statistics, 1563–1801* (Hertfordshire Local History Council, 1964), p. 21. L. Owen, "The Population of Wales in the Sixteenth and Seventeenth Centuries," *Trans. of the Cymmrodorion Society* (1959), p. 113. W. G. Howson, "Plague, Poverty and Population in parts of North-West England, 1580–1720," *Lancs. and Chesh. Hist. Soc. Trans.,* cxii (1960), pp. 29–55.

59. J. F. Pound, "An Elizabethan Census of the Poor," *Univ. of Birmingham Hist. Jl.,* viii (1962), p. 142. P. Laslett, *The World We Have Lost* (London, 1965), p. 69.

60. Hollingsworth, *op. cit.,* p. 25. Laslett, *op. cit.,* p. 83. Stone, *op. cit.,* App. xxxiii and further information from peerage genealogies extracted by Mrs. J. C. Stone. Glass and Eversley, *op. cit.,* pp. 153, 454, 468. P. Styles, "A Census of a Warwickshire Village in 1698," *Univ. of Birmingham Hist. Jl.,* iii (1951), p. 38.

61. Stone, *op. cit.,* pp. 619–23. Glass and Eversley, *op. cit.,* p. 181. Hollingsworth, *op. cit.,* p. 20. Styles, *op. cit.,* p. 40.

62. P. Vincent, "Recherches sur la Fécondité Biologique," *Population,* xvi (1961), p. 111. L. Henry, "La Fécondité Naturelle," *Population,* xvi (1961), p. 633.

63. *V. C. H., Yorks, loc. cit.,* p. 121. Hollingsworth, *op. cit.,* pp. 56–7.

64. Wilson, *England's Apprenticeship, 1600–1763,* p. 352.

65. Hollingsworth, *op. cit.,* pp. 32–4.

66. Stone, *op. cit.,* p. 166.

67. *Op. cit.,* pp. 191, 240–2.

68. The autobiography of the pious London and Boston merchant Robert Keayne is the *locus classicus* of this dilemma: B. Bailyn, ed., *The Apologia of Robert Keayne* (New York, 1965).

69. M. Walzer, *The Revolution of the Saints* (Cambridge, Mass., 1965), *passim.* D. McClelland, *The Achieving Society* (New York, 1961), p. 139.

70. Stone, "Educational Revolution," *loc. cit.*

71. J. Thirsk, "The Sale of Royalist land during the Interregnum," *Econ. Hist. Rev.*, 2nd ser., v. (1952–3), pp. 188–207; and "The Restoration Land Settlement," *Jl. Mod. Hist.*, xxvi (1954), pp. 315–28. H. J. Habakkuk, "Landowners and the Civil War," *Econ. Hist. Rev.*, 2nd ser., xviii [I] (1965), pp. 130–51.

72. Hollingsworth, *op. cit.*, pp. 32–3.

73. Stone, *Crisis*, pp. 30–1.

74. Stone, "Educational Revolution," *loc. cit.* M. 'Espinasse, "The Decline and Fall of Restoration Science," *Past and Present*, no. 14 (Nov., 1958), pp. 71–89.

75. W. E. Tate, *The Parish Chest* (Cambridge, 1946), pp. 18–19. A. Everitt, "Social Mobility in Early Modern England," *Past and Present*, no. 33 (Apr., 1966).

76. A. H. Johnson, *The History of the Worshipful Company of Drapers* (Oxford, 1914–22), ii, pp. 54–5, 197 n. I: iv. pp. 253–4, 634, 643. *V. C. H. Yorks, loc. cit.* pp. 128, 166. W. G. Hoskins, *Provincial England*, p. 109. W. K. Kahl, "Apprenticeship and the Freedom of London Livery Companies, 1690–1750," *Guildhall Miscellany*, vii (1965), pp. 17–20.

77. Barratt, thesis cited note 5, p. 65. Information supplied by Mr. F. S. Odo.

78. Aylmer, *op. cit.*, ch. iii and pp. 263–5.

79. Walzer, *The Revolution of the Saints, passim.*

80. F. L. Ford, *Robe and Sword* (Cambridge, Mass., 1953). P. Goubert, *Beauvais et le Beauvaisis de 1600 à 1730* (Paris, 1960). G. Bluche, *Les Magistrats du Parlement de Paris au XVIIIe siècle* (Paris, 1960). Turgot is quoted by Betty Behrens in *Hist. Jl.*, viii (1965), p. 123.

81. J. Cornwall, "The Early Tudor Gentry," *Econ. Hist. Rev.*, 2nd ser., xvii (1964–5), p. 460. Laslett, *The World We Have Lost*, pp. 62–3.

82. B. E. Supple, *Commercial Crisis and Change in England, 1600–42* (Cambridge, 1959), ch. x. R. Ashton, *The Crown and the Money Market, 1603–40* (Oxford, 1960), pp. 67–78.

83. Laslett, *op. cit.*, pp. 186, 191. P. Styles, "The Heralds' Visitation of Warwickshire in 1682–3," *Birmingham Arch. Soc. Trans.*, lxxi (1953), pp. 131–2. T. C. Mendenhall, *The Shrewsbury Drapers and the Welsh Wool Trade in the Sixteenth and Seventeenth Centuries* (Oxford, 1953), pp. 89–91, and App. C. Calculations from the figures supplied in D. F. Mackensie, "Apprentices in the Stationers' Company, 1555–1640," *The Library*, 5th ser., xiii (1958), pp. 296–7.

84. J. Grant, "The Gentry of London in the Reign of Charles I," *Univ. of Birmingham Hist. Jl.*, viii (1962), pp. 197–201. P. Styles, "The Social Structure of Kineton Hundred . . . ," *Birmingham Arch. Soc. Trans.*, lxxi (1953), p. 106.

85. H. M. Colvin and L. M. Wodehouse, "Henry Bell of King's Lynn," *Architectural History*, iv (1961), pp. 41–62.

86. Styles, "Kineton Hundred," *loc. cit.*, pp. 107–8.

*Large-scale syntheses of necessity minimize local varia-
tions and exceptions. However, before industrialism imposed its great uniformities provincial diversity was
the rule, not the exception. What Joan Thirsk discovers
in this examination of rural England is that there were
not only two Englands of the rich and poor but also
two rural peasant Englands. The first England was the
open field country of corn and sheep agriculture with its
scattered villages dominated by the parish church and the
manor houses of the resident gentry. This rural society was in
trouble economically in the seventeenth century as the price of grain
and wool ceased to rise. But side by side was another England of
pastoral, forest, and fenland agriculture, an increasingly densely
populated rural England which produced a varied and independent
peasantry who turned to industrial by-employment to supplement the
income from their agricultural holdings. The small-holder, whose
gradual disappearance from the corn-growing England was widely
lamented, prospered in the other England, which was already industrialized before the industrial revolution completed its transformation.*

*Dr. Joan Thirsk has been Reader of Economic History in Oxford
University since 1965. Among her publications are* English Peasant
Farming *(London, 1957) and* The Agrarian History of England
and Wales, Vol. IV, 1500–1650 *(Cambridge, 1967), of which she
is editor and part author. The present essay first appeared in* Land,
Church, and People, *ed. Joan Thirsk (Reading, Berks., 1970), pp.
148–177, and is reprinted by permission of the author.*

Seventeenth-Century Agriculture and Social Change

Joan Thirsk

This essay is an attempt to analyse in more detail than hitherto agricultural developments in the seventeenth century, and to present them within a more clearly defined social and geographical framework. The whole century is recognized as a period of economic and political crisis. Agriculturally, this crisis was most readily attributable to the relentlessly falling prices of grain, which posed long-term problems of readjustment to specialized grain growers. But these were only one group among many engaged in agriculture. How did the thousands of farmers who were engaged in other branches of the farming business fare during the seventeenth century? The answer is that some of them met the new circumstances with solutions which were economically successful and far less destructive of the small farmer than those adopted in the specialized corn-growing areas. Thus the farming systems of England became more sharply differentiated economically and socially; and the stage was prepared for changes in the eighteenth century which wrought an agricultural revolution in arable regions and an industrial revolution in pastoral ones.

During the first half of the seventeenth century, fears at the overproduction of grain and its low price commanded the forefront of the stage in all government discussions on agriculture, and particularly during the troubled depression years of 1620–24.[1] In fact, these fears were exaggerated and premature, and they turned to alarms at grain shortage between 1630 and 1632 and in the late 1640s. But the idea of giving some financial encouragement to corn growers was being canvassed by the middle of the century—by Henry Robinson[2] in a pamphlet written in 1652 if not earlier—and after the Restoration farmers were constantly urged to export grain overseas so that corn production could be maintained and its price improved. After 1673 farmers received bounties for so doing.[3] This effort to maintain grain prices proved vain, however, and they fell steadily between 1660 and 1750.[4]

But many corn growers were also wool producers, and in this role they also had cause to complain for low wool prices persisted for most of the century. Rising wool prices which had characterized the sixteenth century were at an end by 1603 and a debate on falling prices had begun by 1610. A sharp crisis accompanied the outbreak of the Thirty Years' War, for it abruptly reduced the demand for cloth in Europe, spreading unemployment among the clothworkers, and quickly reacting upon the wool growers. Thus the shrillest and most alarmist complaints from the countryside in the years 1618–24 came, not surprisingly, from a sheep-corn area, the Lincolnshire wolds, where Sir William Pelham of Brocklesby described small tenants giving up their farms and selling their bed straw for food, eating raw dog flesh and horse flesh for very hunger.[5] It was one of many episodes in the corn-sheep areas which gradually drove the small farmer out of existence.

Grass sheep farmers, however, were almost equally distressed by the cloth crisis, and the complaints of both groups were represented in the report of the Northamptonshire justices of the peace in 1620. Wool, they told the Privy Council, was the chief commodity of the county, yet it would not sell at the lowest price. Compared with this misfortune, the low price of barley was a minor matter; indeed, the latter was rather welcomed since it allayed the discontent of the poor, the "tumultuacious levelling" of 1607 being still green in the memory.[6]

Low wool prices remained a source of anxiety for the rest of the century. Spanish wool was a strong competitor with English wool both at home and overseas. Yet the government insisted in curtailing the market for English wool by prohibiting exports. After the passing of the Irish Cattle Act in 1666, Ireland was forced to turn from cattle to sheep production and her wool also competed successfully against English wool. English wool prices followed a long downward trend after the Restoration, interrupted only during periods of temporary shortage.[7]

Stock farmers and dairymen benefited from a sustained demand for meat and other livestock products which caused prices to maintain a steadier level over the century as a whole.[8] The interests of rearers and graziers were not equally served, however. Already in 1621 the scale of imports of Irish cattle was being criticized as a drain on the bullion reserves of the nation. With butter, they were said to cost £10,000 a year.[9] In the course of the next generation, Irish cattle were increasingly blamed for the stationary or falling level of rents for good grazing land, which seriously hit the incomes of the gentry. Graziers, it was argued, were failing to take up pastures because they were unable to compete with the Irish producers. The remedy adopted at the Restoration was an act in 1663 imposing a duty on imported fat cattle and sheep, followed by the Irish Cattle Act of 1666 which prohibited all livestock imports, both lean and fat, from Ireland. This greatly diminished the supplies of lean stock in England and had the effect of driving up the prices of store animals, greatly to the profit of the rearers of cattle in highland England, Wales, and Scotland. Counties like Devon, Lancashire, and Northumberland benefited at the expense of the graziers in the Midlands and the south, who had to pay higher prices for lean stock than ever before.[10] Thus for a time the profits of meat production were redistributed in favour of the highland rearers at the expense of the lowland graziers. The vociferous complaints against the Irish Cattle Act did not die away until the early 1680s, when in fresh discussions on the merits of the act none could be found to support its repeal.[11] Yet there is no evidence that Midland graziers found the going easier.[12] Around London, however, specialized fattening procedures were evidently producing substantial profits: for example, bullocks which were bought up, stall fed for a year in the Home Counties, and sold fat were yielding high returns while calf fattening was a remunerative speciality in Suffolk and Essex.[13]

Prices of dairy produce, like those of meat, also held up better than grain. In the middle of the century, Sir Richard Weston confidently maintained that the produce of meadows, namely, butter, cheese, tallow, hides, beef, and wool, were all of greater value than corn.[14] But the dairymen were not unaffected by short-term difficulties. From East Anglia they were unable to get their produce away to London by coastal vessels in 1630 because of the

Dunkirk privateers preying on the east coast.[15] The Irish Cattle Act in 1666 caused Irish farmers to turn from cattle production for the English market to dairying whereby they captured English markets for dairy produce in Flanders, France, Portugal, and Spain.[16] This development injured the dairy producers of the south and east, and, according to J. H. Clapham, killed England's export trade in butter.[17] Nevertheless, butter and cheese were easily transported inland, the home demand was insistent, and prices remained stable after 1665.[18] Moreover, in the neighbourhood of towns, and particularly in London, milk sales rose markedly as increasing numbers of pedlars hawked it through the streets. A London milk-woman in the 1690s sold on average sixteen pints of milk a week to each of her customers.[19]

These brief remarks do no more than draw attention to some facets of agricultural development which come to light in contemporary pamphlets, newspapers, and Parliamentary debates. But they are valuable in directing attention at branches of the farming business other than corn growing: each farming type had its own chronology of crises; each crisis threw up different problems for different specialists. Thus, legislation on Irish cattle imports exerted different effects on the rearers of stock (primarily a business of the highland zone of England) and on the graziers (mostly based on the Midlands and south); the evident difficulties of corn producers in selling grain in a saturated market implies differences between the fortunes of farmers cultivating high-grade crops on the most fertile soils and of those producing inferior qualities of grain on the less fertile ones; the hazards of war and changes of policy towards Irish food imports damaged the dairymen of East Anglia and the south at one moment and the West Midlands dairymen at another.[20] And throughout the century it is evident that farmers near towns had a more buoyant market than those at a distance. In short, we can discern differences in the nature and gravity of the seventeenth-century crisis based on geography and farming types.

These, however, are not the only means to a more refined analysis of seventeenth-century agricultural trends. Given the predominance of large farmers in the specialized corn-growing areas and the numerical preponderance of small farmers in pastoral districts, the geographical differences clearly carry social implications as well. And wider perspectives open up when we consider the contemporary literature on agriculture, offering advice to farmers facing the economic problems of their time. Some suggestions, like the growing of vegetables, were immediately within the grasp of the small farmers with little or no capital; others, like the watering of meadows, lay only within the grasp of the rich gentleman or yeoman who could afford to wait years for the full return on his investment. To separate the factors which facilitated agricultural improvements in some places and obstructed them in others, and to measure the ramified consequences of this uneven development, is a complex and ambitious undertaking, especially since farming systems were so numerous and varied. Yet we know that in the end the choices made by different types of farmers shaped conditions in the eighteenth century for an industrial revolution in pastoral areas and an agricultural revolution in arable ones. Thus, as a first step, it should not be impossible to separate, if only in a generalized way, the social and technical factors which changed the structure of English farming regions between 1600 and 1700 and set certain rural communities on paths which diverged ever more sharply after 1750. This should clear the way for local studies which can probe the problem more deeply, and in due course make possible a more far-reaching comparative analysis.

* * *

Specialist corn growers have received most attention from historians because their history is among the best documented and lends itself most readily to generalization. Moreover, bread was a staple food and so bread producers have always been regarded as the central pillar of the farming structure. The growers of high-quality grains for food and drink were found on the wolds and downlands, on the loams and brecks of East Anglia, and in the vales and lowland plains. The life of such communities was centred upon villages which are also deemed typical of the English rural scene. Presided over by the squire, all classes—yeomen, husbandmen, cottagers, labourers, and paupers—were represented in the one community. By the sixteenth or seventeenth centuries, such villages usually lacked any considerable reserves of waste land waiting to be brought into cultivation and so increased production was possible only by intensifying cultivation on the existing land.[21] Much ingenuity was shown in achieving this. A steady increase took place in the proportion of land given to fodder crops, which fed more stock which manured the land more effectively, and so produced more corn. The Lincolnshire hills and vales yield plentiful evidence of this development.[22] In the common fields of Oxfordshire the self-sown leys which were used to feed more stock in the 1630s gave way in the second half of the century to deliberately sown grasses such as rye grass, trefoil, lucerne, clover, and particularly sainfoin.[23] Somewhere between 1650, when Sir Richard Weston wrote his propaganda in favour of clover, and 1662 the price of seed fell from 2s. a pound to 7d. Men had learned to thresh the seed for themselves and no longer relied entirely on Dutch imports. Thus clover became a practical proposition, which Andrew Yarranton could with some assurance recommend to West Midlands farmers below the rank of rich gentleman and yeoman. For this reason, clover spread more widely after the 1660s.[24] At the same time, turnips, which were first popularized as a field crop in Norfolk and Suffolk by the Flemish aliens in the early seventeenth century, were grown more freely on the lighter loams by the middle decades, and, like clover, they improved the performance of the livestock side of arable farming and so indirectly the corn yield.[25]

Meanwhile a search was under way for better varieties of seed that would yield heavier crops of corn. We probably do not know one tenth of the experiments that were going on. Robert Plot wrote of more productive strains of wheat and barley which were cultivated in Oxfordshire and slowly, too slowly for his taste, spread to other counties in the course of the seventeenth century.[26] It is pure luck that Plot happened to record these facts; they must represent a minute proportion of new strains of traditional crops being exploited at this time in the arable centres of England.

The main improvements listed in reply to the questionnaire put out by the Royal Society in 1664 described better rotations in the arable fields, more generous use of fertilizers on the arable, more use of the sheepfold as a fertilizer, and the careful choice of seed.

Questions were put about meadows and pastures but the answers that have survived were brief, and only enumerated the traditional remedies for poor-quality grass.[27] Nevertheless, it was in these corn-growing areas that the watering of meadows took hold in the 1630s, spreading through Wiltshire, Berkshire, Dorset, Hampshire, and later into the Midlands.[28] Like so many of the innovations in corn-growing regions, it is associated with substantial farmers and the owners of great estates. The first watering of meadows by artificial dykes had been devised by Rowland Vaughan, a substantial gentleman farmer living in the Golden Valley of Herefordshire. The digging of the trenches for watering cost him many hundred pounds and it is not surprising that he could not persuade others in the valley to follow his example. His description of his neighbours makes it clear that he lived among small dairymen who were busy with their cheese- and butter-making from May to July and wove hemp and flax in winter. They could not have afforded such expensive innovations.[29] Hence the idea was taken up among wealthier farmers in the corn-growing regions, on the chalk downlands of Salisbury plain where the Earl of Pembroke owned estates, and subsequently in other counties further east. Sir Richard Weston adopted the idea on his lands in Surrey and spent £1,500 on it, not to mention the costs of litigation with his neighbours who claimed damage to their lands by flooding.[30] In Wiltshire Dr. Kerridge has found manor courts agreeing upon co-operative schemes for watering their meadows. But since it remains doubtful how many small husbandmen could have afforded to be involved in such a costly enterprise, it may be that by this time such Wiltshire villages had already succeeded in driving out the small occupier. This would be consonant with Dr. Kerridge's general observation that by 1657 the watering of meadows "was normal amongst gentlemen farmers and cultivating land owners."[31]

Zeal for experiments together with the capital to back them were conspicuous among substantial yeomen and gentry on the most fertile cornlands of the kingdom, and it is no accident that the two outstanding farm account books that have survived from the seventeenth century were written by men farming lands in these districts: Robert Loder at Harwell on the Berkshire downs, and

Henry Best at Elmswell on the Yorkshire wolds.[32] The agricultural revolution of the eighteenth century was likewise publicized by the same class of men farming similar soils. Jethro Tull's *Horse-Hoeing Husbandry* emerged from experience of farming in Berkshire at Crowmarsh Gifford (on the Thames near Wallingford)—superb corn-growing country, producing grain for the London market. After his book was published, Tull moved to a hill farm on the chalk downlands between Berkshire and Wiltshire—an arable, sheep-corn area. Turnip Townshend was similarly concerned with the improvement of potential arable land at Rainham, near Faken-ham, on the brecklands of Norfolk, which when consolidated by sheep and improved by their manure became fertile granaries of corn. Considerably later in the eighteenth century Thomas Coke worked on the same principles in the same countryside.[33]

The logic in this enthusiasm for more intensive arable farming in a period of stagnating prices lay—for farmers on the light lands of the downs and wolds and brecklands, at least—in technical necessi-ty. The sheep-corn system was ideal on these soils and no other commended itself as a substitute. The readiest solution to falling profits, namely, more intensive and more efficient production of the same commodities, was well within the capacity of the large farmer. The consolidation and enclosure of land and the engross-ing of farms were all means to this end. Moreover, by growing more fodder crops, more sheep could be kept on the hills and more cattle in the vales, and thus the sources of income were diversified. In certain geographical situations, other solutions, involving the use of more distant grazing lands as a supplement to the resources of the hill farms, were favoured. Gentlemen farmers on the Lincolnshire wolds and the Kesteven heath rented marshland and fenland to fatten cattle which they could not finish on their home pastures. This practice continued throughout the seventeenth century and only slackened off in the eighteenth when hill farmers recognized the value of growing turnips at home for stock feeding. The renting of these distant pastures was not within the means of the small husbandmen.[34]

In the clay vales farmers had more alternative choices in the changing economic circumstances of the seventeenth century. They were not inescapably tied to corn growing, but could enclose their land and turn it to grass. On heavy soils this was an attractive solution, particularly as it solved the problem posed by high wages, of which lowland farmers generally complained in the second half of the seventeenth century.[35] "Pasturage is more profitable than tillage," wrote one pamphleteer in 1654, "why should they [i.e., the enclosing farmers] not have liberty to lay down their arable land for grass."[36] In fact, they continued to do just this in many parts of the East Midlands—in Leicestershire, Northamptonshire, and north Buckinghamshire. It is roughly estimated that nearly a quarter of Leicestershire was enclosed in the seventeenth century.[37] The pamphlet controversy for and against enclosure between two Leicestershire parsons, John Moore and Joseph Lee, in 1653–54 seems something of an anachronism in seventeenth-century England—for public opinion was generally moving in favour of enclosure so long as it safeguarded the interests of the poor commoners—yet it did not appear so in the East Midlands; here enclosure was still a lively present issue.[38]

There is general agreement among those who have worked on particular parishes and estates in the arable districts of England that these economic changes caused land to become more and more concentrated in the hands of the larger farmers. A H. Johnson, who many years ago sought to explain the decline of the small landowners, found evidence for it between the sixteenth and the mid-eighteenth centuries, and more particularly between 1688 and 1750, in Oxfordshire parishes generally, and on various estates in Norfolk, Sussex, Kent, Wiltshire, the Isle of Wight, and Leicestershire.[39] It is noticeable that his evidence was drawn from the best corn-growing regions. His comparisons were of a rough and ready kind, but the difficulties in estimating changes in the number of owner-occupiers during the seventeenth century have discouraged others from attempting other large comparisons. Most modest examples from single parishes, however, have shown the same trends.

At Sherington in Buckinghamshire, for example, modest free-holders who had been gaining ground in the late sixteenth century when manorial lords sold out their interests, and who continued to flourish until the 1660s, were driven out by indebtedness between 1660 and 1710. The engrossing of holdings proceeded apace and

many merchants and town dwellers became owners.[40] At Chippenham in Cambridgeshire, where the common fields were not enclosed until 1791, large farms nevertheless grew at the expense of
the rest during the seventeenth century. Circumstances in this case
suggest that it was not always debt that drove men to sell. Rents
were falling, and the weight of taxation borne by owners of land
was rising. Since there were sound arguments for becoming a
tenant rather than an owner in the second half of the seventeenth
century, the three Chippenham farmers who sold out farms of
between 120 and 155 acres apiece in 1696 to enable the lord to
create a park may have made their choice deliberately and
willingly.[41]

Some gentle propaganda in favour of small farms began to flow
in the late sixties and early seventies from people familiar with
conditions in the lowland zone who viewed with increasing anxiety
the fall of rents. Sir Thomas Culpeper, Jr., in the preface which he
wrote in 1668 to his father's *Tract against the High Rate of Usury*,
described the increase of large farms as more appropriate to New
England than Old England, and mourned the diminution of small
ones. Carew Reynel believed that "the smaller estates the land is
divided into the better for the nation, the more are maintained,
and the land better husbanded."[42]

The decline of the small landowner in the seventeenth century,
then, was a feature of specialized arable regions, and also of vale
lands newly enclosed for pasture, not, as we shall see presently, of
traditional pasture-farming districts. The smaller farmer was being
driven out by a combination of factors, notably the technical
economies possible in large-scale cereal production, or in conver-
sions to pasture, sluggish grain prices, and the high cost and
quantity of labour in corn growing. Capital was essential both to the
farmers who chose to intensify grain production and to those who
chose to turn over entirely to grazing. Nor surprisingly, it was from
among these farmers, and not from the ancient pasture-farming
communities, that the livestock improvers like Robert Bakewell and
the Culley brothers emerged in the eighteenth century.[43] They had
been nurtured in communities so structured as to promote the
interests of the thrusting and ambitious improver.

This generalized conspectus of arable-farming regions in the seventeenth century takes its guidelines from the examples of the best corn-growing lands and the most ordered village communities. It omits certain variants: these were the villages with less fertile soils which continued under arable cultivation without yielding great rewards to their cultivators; crops other than corn could quickly win general favour if they prospered in the environment. The variant villages, socially speaking, were those which lacked the controlling influence of a squire, either because the ownership of land was divided among several lords of almost equal status, or because the village entirely lacked a lord (this could occur if the manorial rights were sold up and the manorial courts ceased to be held), or because the manorial lord allowed things to slide through sheer negligence. Many such communities maintained a strong freeholder class, which ruled the village when necessary, but which failed, often from self-interest, to check the influx of immigrant cottagers and squatters. These became the "open" villages of the eighteenth century, providing much-needed casual labour for the farmers in the "closed" villages roundabout. Wigston Magna, Leicestershire, is one such example: it solved the problem of employment for its inhabitants by turning to framework knitting, which was already entrenched in forest areas nearby, and which spread in the second half of the seventeenth century into the almost equally congenial environment afforded by such "open" villages.[44] Industries, however, were not the only solution to the problem of employment in such communities. Another solution lay in the cultivation of special, labour-intensive crops.

Pamphlet literature during the seventeenth century recommended with growing conviction and growing precision the cultivation of specialized cash crops, commanding a high and profitable price at the markets. These were fruit and vegetables; herbs and spices for cooking and medicinal purposes, such as saffron, caraway, mustard, and liquorice; industrial dyes such as woad, weld, madder, and safflower; flax and hemp for cloth weaving; mulberries for feeding silkworms; and teasels, which were used for brushing up the nap of cloth and were considerably cheaper than wire cards. The first exhortations to grow these crops were made by men who had travelled in European countries, particularly Flanders and France, and drew object lessons from their observations. Some were cloth merchants who readily saw the commercial advantages of producing flax, hemp, and dyes at home instead of importing them; others were gentlemen who collected unusual plants and foods for their gardens and dining tables and either bought them from special importers in London or sent their gardeners abroad to collect them.[45]

The lessons were only slowly driven home. When the example of the Dutch was preached to Englishmen in the early 1620s as a model to be copied for alleviating the economic crisis, the cultivation of flax, hemp, and tobacco at home were principally commended as a means of saving on foreign imports. The obvious remedies for the sick economy at that time seemed to lie in increasing the volume of trade and improving the money supply.[46] By the middle of the century, however, proposals for overcoming a new and even deeper depression were far more broadly conceived, and gave a prominent place to schemes for the diversification of agriculture. The need to provide more employment for the poor loomed large, and, with the objective in mind, political writers set great store by labour-demanding crops which would increase work on the land and indirectly in industry. Thus Henry Robinson's pamphlet in 1652 entitled *Certain Proposals in order to the People's Freedom and Accommodation* wished to foster weaving industries of silk, cotton, hemp, and flax as well as wool, and to grow most of these fibres at home. To provide additional land for them he urged the more productive use of wastes, which meant, of course, enclosure as a first step. But so long as the commoners' interests were protected, Robinson believed this to be a desirable improvement.[47] These two arguments in combination became standard among writers on the economy during the Interregnum and for the rest of the century. Flax and hemp would increase the variety and quantity of domestic handicrafts; dye crops required much hand labour and would also save the cost of imported dyes; vegetables and fruit used land and labour intensively, were in great demand, and extremely profitable. Changes in dietary habits had occurred during the civil wars and people now ate only one main meal a day, consuming less meat and eating more fruit and vegetables.[48] Sales in towns were brisk: Londoners of all classes bought fruit from pedlars and munched it in the streets—like goats, the Venetian Busoni remarked unkindly.[49]

The literature advocating these crops was voluminous after 1650 and cannot be recited in detail. But two editions of Walter Blith's textbook on husbandry serve as signposts to the success of the propaganda. In 1649, Blith published *The English Improver or a New Survey of Husbandry*, and enumerated "six pieces of improvement." These were (i) the floating and watering of land, (ii) the draining of fens, bogs, and marshland, (iii) the ploughing of old pasture, and enclosure without depopulation, (iv) the careful use of manures appropriate to different soils, (v) the planting of woods, and (vi) the more modest improvement of lands presenting special problems. In 1652 the new edition of this work, entitled *The English Improver Improved*, contained the same recommendations but added "six newer pieces of improvement." These were (i) the growing of clover, sainfoin, and lucerne, (ii) the correct use of ploughs appropriate to different soils, (iii) the planting of weld, woad, and madder, (iv) the planting of hops, saffron, and liquorice, (v) the cultivation of rape, coleseed, hemp, and flax, and (vi) the planting of orchard and garden fruits. In the revised text Blith implied that some at least of these new crops had only just been brought to his notice, perhaps, we may guess, as a result of comments by readers of the first edition. Of weld, he wrote with a trace of pique, "it is my desire to make public whatever comes under my experience, yet this hath been used this many years by many private gentlemen in divers parts but not discovered for public practice. . . . I fear men's spirits are strangely private that have made excellent experiments and yet will not communicate."[50]

Where and by whom were these crops adopted and how did they relieve the problems of corn-growing communities in the seventeenth century? The dye crops, vegetables, fruits, herbs, and spices were all taken up with alacrity in arable areas. For technical reasons, the dye crops did not generally commend themselves to small growers, and, except in market gardens, were cultivated by more substantial farmers with capital, and even by adventurers who moved around the country renting land for short periods at high prices.[51] Madder, for example, took three years to mature and yield its first crop. Moreover, the best plants had to be brought from Zealand or at least bought in London from an importer. After three years of waiting, the grower preferably needed access to a madder mill for drying and pounding, although as an alternative he could employ women and children to do the job by hand during the winter. At all events, he faced strong competition from the Dutch product, for Zealand madder was noted for its high quality and was imported in quantity. Nevertheless, if successful, madder could yield a profit of £300 an acre after three years, and £160 for an indifferent crop.[52]

The early attempts at madder growing in England are associated with a London dyer, Mr. Minne, who evidently had the capital to invest in a long-term project. Around 1620 he sent George Bedford to study its secrets in the Netherlands and spent £1,000 in nine years keeping him there. When Bedford returned with some plants, he tried to grow them in Romney Marsh, a significant choice of district, for it was a happy hunting ground for outsiders who leased land in the seventeenth century and did not reside there.[53] Another adventurer with madder was Sir Nicholas Crisp, who set up a madder plantation at Deptford. Later in the century it was grown for a short while near Wisbech, but since Wisbech lies on the edge of the Bedford Level, we may fairly suspect that this was an enterprise promoted not by traditional fen peasants but by some of the big farmers who came into the Level after drainage and took up large tracts of land as a speculative venture.[54] The only madder growing which was carried on on a small scale occurred in market gardens around towns and mainly around cloth-working centres. Growers cultivated vegetables such as cabbage, kidney beans, radishes, onions, and herbs between the madder plants to yield a harvest in the years before the madder was ready, and since both kinds of plants need continuous weeding, this system worked well.[55]

Woad was another dye which required capital and had to be grown on a large scale if it was to yield the best profit. "Experiments of a little parcel," wrote Walter Blith, were useless; one must grow enough to keep at least one mill at work. It also made heavy demands on labour during the summer for two weedings and at least two cuttings in mid-June and mid-July. Thus clothiers disliked it because it made labour short for spinning in summer. It was therefore not well suited to pastoral areas where the cloth industry was entrenched, and much better suited to arable-farming systems where a summer supply of casual labour was already at hand. In these conditions it was one of the most rewarding crops of any. "The best estates that hath been got in all our rich upland countries," maintained Walter Blith, "have been got by it [i.e., woad]." By this he meant estates in the Midland countries of Northamptonshire, Leicestershire, Rutland, Felden Warwickshire, Oxfordshire, parts of Worcestershire, and Gloucestershire, and in Bedfordshire and Buckinghamshire where woad was incorporated in a system of alternate husbandry, being a good first crop when pasture was being broken up for corn. Its other home was in gardens, particularly around cloth towns such as Godalming, Farnham, and Winchester.[56]

A dye crop which found a congenial home on upland arable farms was weld, producing a bright yellow dye. It prospered on chalky barren hillsides wherever the soil was warm and dry. Thus it was widely grown on the downlands around Canterbury and Wye where it was inserted into the arable rotation, being sown in with barley or oats one year for a harvest the following year. It did not call for much cultivation while growing, though it was a "ticklish vegetable" prone to blasting and to other accidents if bad weather damaged it in spring. When harvested the stalks simply had to be dried and some of the seed shaken out for the next year's crop. It was a plant which diversified the interests of sheep-corn farmers without posing any special problems of cultivation and harvesting.[57]

A new dye crop which gained ground notably in the 1660s and 1670s was safflower or bastard saffron. It yielded a reddish pink dye and was much in demand from the silk dyers, who had hitherto obtained the bulk of their supplies from around Strasbourg in Germany. It was an indigenous English plant but it began to be grown more deliberately around London, in Gloucestershire, and in Oxfordshire in an effort to undercut the price of the imported article. Successful growers found it extremely profitable, yielding clear gains of £20–£30 per acre in a year; its only disadvantage was that it was harvested at the same time as wheat. Thus it is not clear whether it was adopted by pasture farmers or was taken up by arable farmers with unusually ample supplies of casual labour during the summer.[58]

Saffron was a traditional English crop which feared no competitors. It was deemed far superior in quality to any of foreign origin.

Its chief use was medicinal, demand was high, and it commanded good prices. It was grown in arable fields, even in common fields, in Suffolk, Essex, and Cambridgeshire, and also in Herefordshire. It called for much hand labour, first in setting the roots in trenches, and then in gathering the saffron every morning for about a month in summer. Clear profit ranged from £3.10s. to over £30 an acre.[59]

Another special crop was liquorice, which was grown around towns where plenty of dung was available. Since it stayed in the ground for three summers before the roots grew to any size, vegetables such as onions, leeks, and lettuces were cultivated in between. It was grown in quantity around London, at Godalming in Surrey, at Pontefract in Yorkshire, and around Worksop in Nottinghamshire. In the words of John Parkinson, the herbalist, writing in 1640 it "is much used nowadays to be planted in great quantity even to fill many acres of ground, whereof riseth a great deal of profit to those that know how to order it and have fit grounds for it to thrive in." At the end of the century profits of £50-£100 an acre were quoted in exceptional cases.[60]

Market gardeners have already appeared in this account as growers of dyes and medicinal crops. But vegetables and fruit were their main livelihood and contemporary descriptions leave no doubt of the remarkable success of this specialized branch of farming. Vegetable seeds were cheaply and easily bought from seedsmen in London and other towns and from country innkeepers.[61] The land required was small, and every foot was profitably used; fruit trees separated the beds of vegetables. The towns which devoured the produce readily supplied dung for the next season's crops. In short, horticulture was ideally suited to small peasants with little land, no capital, but plenty of family labour, and with easy access to a town. Good market-garden land fetched high rents, but vegetables could be grown on poorer land, richly dunged, and were sown on many strips in common fields. While good-quality produce fetched handsome prices, better returns still came from the cultivation of vegetables for seed.[62] Four or five acres of land used in this way, declared John Houghton, would sometimes maintain a family better and employ more labourers than fifty acres of other land; £100 from an acre was thought a not impossible return.[63]

The prosperity of the market gardeners along Thames-side is

well known but they also throve in many other districts of the Home Counties and, indeed, all over southern England in the neighbourhood of busy towns. Tewkesbury, for example, produced excellent carrots, which were distributed to markets via the Avon and the Severn. In Surrey the gardeners were clustered on the Lower Greensand, on the Bagshot Beds, and on alluvial soils in the valleys of the rivers Mole and Wey. In consequence, the whole county was especially renowned for its "gardening for profit," a reputation which is reflected in numerous tithe disputes relating to vegetables and also to hops, the latter being extensively grown around Godalming and Farnham. A dispute in 1687 at Farnham listed twenty-two people in the parish growing hops and this did not claim to be a complete list. Witnesses alleged that there were forty owners or occupiers of land planted with hops and that they covered between 250 and 300 acres of land. The tithe owners evidently shared handsomely in the benefits for the tithe of six and a half acres of hops was said to be valued at £15.[64]

Books on horticulture found a ready sale in the second half of the seventeenth century. French works were translated into English and Englishmen wrote their own handbooks, "wrung out of the earth" as one reviewer put it. The work to which this description was particularly applied was *The Garden of England* by Sir Hugh Platt, which incorporated much that he had learned by diligent correspondence and assiduous visits to gardeners around London. Clubs of experts were formed in London, where men received the latest information from other parts of the country and from Europe, and being "apt to essay novelties and rarities" they turned this knowledge to good account.[65]

The intensity of cultivation in the best organized market gardens is illustrated in the probate inventory of Robert Gascoine, a gardener of St. Martin in the Fields, who died in February 1718. He had row upon row of cauliflower and cabbage plants—1,000 plants were set in two banks three rows wide—radishes, carrots, colewort, young lettuce, asparagus, onions, spinach, and artichokes, while fruit trees lined the palings between the beds. Forty rods of asparagus were of the first year's planting, 124 rods were one year old, and 32 rods were ready for cutting, with colewort in the alleys between. In addition, other beds of asparagus and lettuce were being forced under glass. The surname of this gardener strongly suggests a French immigrant, but if his expertise and the scale of his enterprise placed him in the first rank of market gardeners, he was not alone. Other gardeners' inventories show the same system in operation, their crops being sometimes more specialized and sometimes less. John Lee of St. Martin in the Fields, dying in July 1684, had specialized in asparagus and cucumber as well as growing cherry and other fruit trees between the beds. Curtis Akers of Chelsea in April 1686 was growing herbs, asparagus, carrots, parsnips, and beans. Another gardener in St. Martin in the Fields in February 1682 grew only asparagus.[66]

This evidence does not give any clue to the total volume of production, nor can we compare the value of vegetables, fruit, and other special crops with the grain, meat, and dairy produce sent to the market by other farmers.[67] But the weight of contemporary comment leaves no doubt that specialists in these branches of farming weathered the crisis of the seventeenth century with ease. By 1670 Sir William Coventry put the argument in their favour in the simplest cash terms: corn and cattle were being produced to excess and the population was not increasing rapidly enough to consume it all. The solutions to this dilemma were to sell the surplus abroad (corn bounties, in fact, followed soon afterwards), or to increase the population consuming it at home, or to divert land from corn and meat to the growing of other crops, the ones which he most favoured being woad, flax, and hemp.[68] Farming textbooks in the second half of the seventeenth century consistently gave specialized cash crops their full share of space and added circumstantial details on yields, labour costs, and the net profit. The correspondence columns of John Houghton's weekly journal, *A Collection for the Improvement of Husbandry and Trade*, contained frequent homilies on their advantages; and the current market prices of saffron, caraway seed, linseed, and mustard were quoted regularly between 1694 and 1697.[69]

Except for hemp and flax, which are dealt with below in the account of pasture-farming regions, all these specialized crops were the produce of arable-farming regions. As we have seen, some were taken up by the market gardeners and other small growers, others were adopted by wealthier and bolder spirits who were prepared to invest capital and take risks, and were assured of adequate casual labour in busy seasons. Such pools of labour were most readily at hand in "open" villages and it was doubtless in the neighbourhood of such communities that the most successful enterprises were established and maintained.

Further work will undoubtedly yield instructive illustrations of the association between labour-intensive crops and overpopulous villages in arable regions. An example from a town in Gloucestershire, however, gives a vivid example of this association, arising through unusual circumstances in a pastoral area. "Open" communities were not, of course, confined to arable districts; but their labour problems stood out most conspicuously in the latter case because they contrasted strongly with the "closed" villages roundabout and because the two types complemented each other economically. There were "open" villages in pastoral regions, but, as we shall see below, they did not present employment problems that were any different in kind from those of all other pastoral communities. Under-employment was common to them all.

Winchcombe was a market town in the pastoral vale of Gloucester. Its markets had fallen into decay, and it may thus be presumed to have had an economy that was hardly different from that of a village, though its population was larger. Tobacco growing took firm hold, as it did in many other villages in Worcestershire and Gloucestershire. Moreover, the lord of the manor failed to hold any courts or to enforce the bylaws, and uncontrolled immigration into Winchcombe followed. Single family houses were divided into tenements to accommodate two, three, and four families. The houses fell into disrepair and were in danger of falling into the street. Lodgers and beggars thronged the place: according to the poor-law overseers there were twenty households of paupers begging for alms for every household able to bestow them. The lord of the manor attempted to remedy this state of affairs in 1662 by imposing entry fines for the first time in many years, and met with indignant resistance from his tenants. The dispute of 1662 was thus concerned with an inquiry into the customs of Winchcombe. "Hath not the neglect of executing the orders and bylaws upon offenders much encouraged the people there to become careless of offending in taking in of inmates and undertenants?"

asked the Exchequer commissioners. This was clearly one of the causes of the trouble. But it is impossible for us not to see some association between tobacco growing and the inordinate growth of Winchcombe's population. The lord of the manor had neglected to control movement into the town. The trade of the market was declining. Tobacco was a labour-intensive crop which offered work and cash to all comers. People had crowded into Winchcombe for cheap accommodation and jobs, and the prohibition on the growing of tobacco after 1619 had not noticeably detracted from its popularity. The planters paid fines and later excise and continued to grow it. In 1652 an Act prohibited tobacco growing afresh, but it was followed by yet another in 1653 allowing offenders to pay excise and quietly harvest their crops. Not so in 1654. The Council of State took the legislation more seriously this time and sent soldiers to destroy the crop. Winchcombe people raised three hundred armed horse and foot to resist the attack, declaring that they were bred to the trade, and "if they lose it they will lose their lives." Signatories to a petition to Cromwell from Winchcombe tobacco growers numbered 110 persons.[70]

Tobacco growing was not stamped out until the late 1670s. Winchcombe was left in a pitiful plight, overpopulated and without adequate work. Its inhabitants subsequently resorted to stocking knitting. A visitor passing through the town in 1678 remarked upon the sight of the women folk carrying their puddings and bread to the common bakehouse, smoking and knitting as they went.[71]

In this account of arable-farming systems in the seventeenth century, three main streams of development may be discerned. On the best corn-growing lands, the large farmers prospered, offsetting the fall of grain prices by growing more grain with greater efficiency and driving out the small growers. In the vales, events followed the same course, except that in some places arable farms were converted into pasture for feeding cattle and keeping sheep. The work that was provided for the agricultural labourer was little enough on pasture farms[72] and liable to sudden interruption on arable ones. On suitable land less fertile for corn, special cash crops were grown by men with capital who could rely on the plentiful supply of casual labour from "open" villages. However, the Diggers

in Surrey, Kent, Northamptonshire, and Buckinghamshire who
dug up the commons in 1649 during deep economic depression
expressed the resentment of many poor labourers in arable areas
when misfortune hit their employers and left them both landless
and workless.[73] As for the small farmer in arable areas, he had little
hope of survival, except in those districts which were suited to
market gardening. Here, indeed, he had positive advantages over
his richer and larger competitor.

*   *   *

It remains for us to consider how the peasantry fared in pastoral
regions. The pasture-farming regions present a different set of
social and geographical circumstances. Grass growing was the
primary objective of all farmers but their ultimate goals were
varied, and may be broadly grouped under four headings: in the
mountains and moorlands of northern England and on the moorlands of the south-west, cattle and sheep were reared; in the vales
of the West Midlands and in other areas where the heavy soils lay
under permanent grass, dairying was one speciality, rearing and
fattening, sometimes in combination, were the others. In forest
areas horse breeding and pig fattening played an important role
alongside stock keeping; in the fenlands of eastern England and
the Somerset Level stock enterprises were mixed.[74]

Pasture farmers lived in isolated farms and hamlets as well as in
villages, and the population was thus more widely scattered than in
the arable lowlands. Manorial courts could not exercise close
surveillance over their tenants, and tenants generally held their
land by freer tenures. In many of these dispersed centres of
settlement, moreover, it is noticeable that the population consisted
of one class only; the poor and the rich did not always live cheek by
jowl, as in the nucleated villages. In Staffordshire, for example, it is
remarkable how many hamlets recorded in the Hearth Tax Return
of 1666 consisted either of the rich or of the poor but not of both.
In fact in many parishes, some of which had ten or fourteen
separate settlements, it was ususal to find that half the townships
mixed the classes, while in the other half they lived firmly segre-
gated. All in all, the inhabitants enjoyed much greater freedom and
this bred in them a fiery spirit of independence, which armed them

for struggle. As one nineteenth-century writer expressed it, when comparing this life favourably with that of the inhabitants of the squire's village, "a dominant and resident landowner was the centre of intelligence, of charity, and of social life," but for these advantages there was a social price to pay. "It is as true in the parish as in the nation that a paternal government makes a childish people. A man whose brothers and neighbours are dependent upon him is prone to become overbearing whilst the neighbours and even the brothers are apt to become obsequious." There was little danger of this in the pastoral districts of the kingdom.[75]

The seventeenth century was a testing time for pasture farmers living in fens and forests. Strife and controversy had surrounded enclosure and engrossing in the arable regions for more than a hundred years. Now the pastoral areas came under attack from the agricultural improvers. "Improvement of the wastes and forests" became the slogan of the age. The Crown led the way in the early decades of the century with its schemes for the drainage of the fens and disafforestation of the forests, in both of which countrysides it had considerable landed interests. The principal investors in, and beneficiaries from, its schemes were members of the Court circle, nobility, and gentry, as well as the drainers and their friends. The native peasantry had nothing to gain and much to lose by their designs, for in both forests and fens they were intended to turn pastoral economies into arable ones, and would inevitably have altered the structure of the local communities. The agricultural system in pastoral areas prospered on the basis of certain well-defined conditions. Society was dominated by family farmers; the economy depended on imports of corn from other districts, the use of spacious commons for feeding stock, and the availability of supplementary work in industries of many kinds. The drainers in the fens and the improvers disafforesting the forests did not fully appreciate that the destruction of the old economies meant the destruction of their societies as well; the inhabitants, on the other hand, perceived this instinctively. Most of the riots in the years before the Civil War (though not the Midland Revolt of 1607) broke out in pastoral and forest areas, threatened by changes which undermined their whole way of life. The worst outbreaks occurred in the years 1629–32, when the three pillars of the

economy—imported corn, spacious commons, and domestic industries—threatened to crumble simultaneously. First bad weather hit
the pasture farmers, creating a shortage of hay and cattle feed, and
spreading cattle murrain among their herds. Then it spoiled the
corn harvests in 1630 and 1632 and made it impossible for some
pastoral communities to buy corn at any price. Plague took hold in
1631. And acute unemployment hit the domestic, and particularly
the cloth, industries. "Want of work," bad weather, and the
intrusions of drainers and improvers hit the pastoral areas with
unprecedented harshness. Hence the many riots in the pastoral
and forest districts of Wiltshire, Dorset, Hampshire, Gloucestershire, Worcestershire, and Rutland.[76]

The conviction that improvement of the wastes and forests was
the first priority in agriculture persisted if anything more strongly
during the Interregnum than under the early Stuarts.[77] The only
difference was that writers hedged their recommendations about
with safeguards for the commoners. "Improvement" had become a
dirty word. "Scarce anyone," wrote John Houghton later on
recalling these years, "durst offer for improvements lest he should
be called a Projector as if he came from the fens to borrow 5s. to
purchase £5,000 yearly, so averse were our English then from all
care of improvements."[78] The angry commoners instilled a fear
which lingered well beyond Houghton's time. It still permeated the
atmosphere of debates in the House of Lords on the draining of
fens in 1701 and 1711. The plan to enclose and drain was called
"the most arbitrary proceeding in the world. It invades the properties of thousands of people."[79]

The vision which inspired would-be improvers of forests, fens,
and chases during the Interregnum was the prospect of increasing
employment. One fifth more people, argued Silvanus Taylor,
might be fed if waste lands were enclosed. But he did not plan or
predict the class structure of such communities. The experiments
which were brought to conclusion in the fens created large farms
running into hundreds of acres, occupied by strangers rather than
local inhabitants, including many Dutchmen.[80] Thus the crisis of
the seventeenth century in these regions was created by short-
sighted planners with an obsessive predilection for corn-growing
economies, blind to the looming economic difficulties of corn

growers elsewhere, and wilfully ignoring the fact that corn-growing systems fostered large farms far more successfully than they
sustained small peasants. Their schemes were designed to create
class-divided communities of the lowland kind with their due
proportion of yeomen, husbandmen, labourers, and paupers,
presided over by an affluent gentleman. Fortunately, they did not
succeed in moulding much of pastoral England in the image of the
arable lowlands.

Outside these disturbed areas, agricultural improvements by
pasture farmers were necessarily made at modest cost, did not
generally disturb neighbours, and thus leave less trace in our
records. The social obstacles to expensive capital improvements
have already been illustrated in the experiences of Rowland
Vaughan, who devised the scheme for watering meadows in the
Golden Valley of Herefordshire. He cheerfully spent large sums in
order to get his young lambs ready for the butcher a month before
his competitors. His neighbours, on the other hand, who were
family farmers, dairying in the summer and weaving hemp and
flax in the winter, pursued another course of life altogether.[81]

Despite the difficulties, described by Andrew Yarranton, in
spreading innovations among farmers without much spare cash for
experiments that could easily fail, stock in pasture-farming areas
benefited from the ley grasses that were improving the feed of
animals in arable areas. In general, however, they continued to be
fed mainly on grass and hay, though care was devoted to the
improvement of the herbage by careful grazing, frequent cutting
down of thistles, rushes, etc., and by the application of dung, lime,
potash, and ashes, and by drainage with open or covered drains.
These measures, which feature prominently in the replies to the
Georgical inquiries in 1664, were all traditional, but they nevertheless produced substantial improvements in the feeding capacity of
pastures. Walter Blith in 1652 particularly extolled the efforts of
farmers in the woodland parts, "as in Worcestershire, Warwickshire, Staffordshire, Shropshire, and Wales-ward and northward,"
in improving their coarse lands by these traditional methods. He
judged the land to be as highly improved as many parts of the
fielden country *and fuller of wealthier inhabitants.*"[82]

Little evidence survives concerning the selection and care of stock; but the social structure of pastoral communities affords part of the explanation. They did not produce men who kept accounts or had the flair for publicly advertising their achievements. Samuel Hartlib complained in 1651 that "we advance not the best species," but it is not clear which farmers he had in mind; and he did single out for measured praise the pasture farmers of Lancashire and some other northern counties who "are a little careful in these particulars."[83] What is clear is that the pastoral regions, as the main breeding centres for stock, had been responsible for developing a remarkable number of different breeds of cattle, sheep, and horses, which were adapted to suit different environments. If a man changed the environment by improving his land, then he could change the breed of his animals, as farmers of enclosed pastures in the sixteenth century evidently changed the breeds of sheep which they kept.

If we look in vain for spectacular innovations and the willingness to invest capital such as that which possessed corn growers like Henry Best, Jethro Tull, and others, this does not mean that the populations of pastoral areas were living in a derelict and miserable backwater, outside the main stream of enterprise. Traditionally, pastoral areas were the abode of small family farmers and their way of life suited their environment. The common pastures were a community asset available to all, and many farming systems, like dairying and pig keeping, required small capital. But another key to the success of this way of life, which enabled men to weather successfully the seventeenth-century crisis, was the many additional opportunities for earning a living. Some simply involved exploiting the diversity of natural resources: fishing, fowling, cutting reeds for thatching and for fuel in the fens; timber felling and the manufacture of woodware in the forests. Mining offered work in some areas; in others there were domestic industries such as potting, nail-making, metal-working, lace-making, stocking knitting, and the weaving of woollen, linen, and hempen cloth. In some districts the growth of flax and hemp weaving was facilitated by larger imports of the raw material from the Baltic which was more widely distributed inland as rivers were improved. Nidderdale in West Yorkshire and parts of Derbyshire, for example, enjoyed an easy link with the port of Hull.[84] In other counties the domestic weaving of hemp and flax went hand in hand with an increase in the cultivation of these crops. Some of the propaganda in favour of growing them was directed at counties lacking adequate domestic industries, such as Leicestershire, Northamptonshire, and Oxfordshire.[85] In fact, however, it was in pastoral areas where handicraft industries were already well established that it spread most successfully, particularly in the West Midlands, in parts of Herefordshire, Worcestershire, Warwickshire, Nottinghamshire, Derbyshire, and Staffordshire.[86] Staffordshire, indeed, was described by Robert Sharrock as exemplary in its system of growing these two crops; and it seems legitimate to argue from the increasing references in this county to tithes of hemp and flax in the later seventeenth and early eighteenth centuries that production was expanding.[87] Other pastoral areas which grew flax and hemp were the marshlands of Thames-side in Essex and Kent, the fens of eastern England and the Somerset Level, parts of Dorset, the Weald of Kent around Maidstone, which was the renowned thread-making centre of the kingdom, and the forests of Northamptonshire. When Sir Richard Weston came back from the Netherlands urging flax growing, he recommended experiments in St. Leonards Forest in Sussex.[88] Like the industrial crops which flourished in arable regions, hemp and flax were universally regarded as profitable ventures: some hemp and flax ground was rented for £3 an acre, labour costs added another £2 or £3, but the crop was worth £10–£12. Thus profits were in the region of £5–£6 an acre.[89]

In pastoral regions farming combined with industrial employment was almost common form. The combination was well integrated into a life focused on the family as the wage-earning group. The nailer's forge and the pottery were sheds next door to the farmhouse, while the weaving loom might be in the parlour or chamber or in separate weaving shed.[90] A rare glimpse of the detailed programme of daily life is offered in the diary of a farmer-weaver in 1782-83 who worked out of doors one day till three o'clock and then wove two yards of cloth before sunset. On wet days he might weave eight and a half to nine yards. One Christmas Eve he wove two yards before 11 A.M. and spent the rest of the day doing winter jobs around the house and midden. In addition, he had occasional work on other people's farms, hauling timber, preparing a calf stall, fetching and carrying with his own horse and cart, and picking cherries.[91] The variety of work compensated for the absence of some material comforts. Indeed, the use of the term "by-employments" for the industrial occupations of pasture farmers may convey a false impression. They were not accidental or subsidiary, secondary, or a miserable makeshift. They were an integral part of the pastoral way of life. They remain so in many pastoral regions of England, though the numbers of people so occupied form such a small proportion of the total population that they are not seriously considered.[92] But in countries where peasant-workers still represent a much larger slice of the population, this way of life is recognized and studied as a permanent social and economic phenomenon with merits of its own. In Poland, for example, it is agreed that the family budget of the peasant-worker at the present time is decidedly larger than that of the farmer of a medium-sized holding with only his land to support him.[93] In England today it is reasonable to regard the peasant-worker as a negligible element in rural society, but not so in the seventeenth century. Indeed, we may guess that such farmers must have comprised somewhere near half the farming population of the kingdom. The economy and fortunes of this group deserve more attention than has yet been given to them for theirs is a different story with a different chronology from that of the small owner-occupier and small tenant in arable regions.

It is too early to make dogmatic generalized statements about the economic fortunes of traditional pasture-farming areas in the seventeenth century or about the size of their populations. But there are suggestive clues to some economic trends. Multiple sources of income attracted immigrants to the pastoral areas. Numerous contemporaries remarked (usually with disapproval) on this migration, particularly into the forests and fens of the Midland, southern, and eastern counties. Against this background the Act of Settlement in 1662 takes on a special significance. Its preamble refers to the movement of people from parish to parish "to settle themselves where there is the best stock, the largest commons or wastes to build cottages, and the most woods for them to burn and destroy." Roger Coke, writing eight years after the passing of this Act, believed it to be without effect: squatters on the waste were increasing daily.[94]

In some places we can measure a substantial growth of population at least until the Act of Settlement. In others it continued into the early eighteenth century. In part of the Lincolnshire fenland, for example, numbers almost doubled between 1563 and 1723, whereas in arable parts of the same county the population at these two dates was more or less the same. Warwickshire figures of average populations in arable and forest areas do not illustrate growth rates but they do demonstrate the larger populations living in the forests: the average size of communities in old enclosed arable parishes in 1663 was forty-six households, in unenclosed arable parishes fifty-four households, and in pastoral (Arden) parishes 120 households.[95]

Professor Everitt's comparison of labourers with less than an acre of land in the period 1500–1640 shows a considerably higher proportion in fielden parishes (72 percent) than in fell parishes (65 percent) or forest parishes (44 percent), and, of course, in fell and forest regions the common rights that went with land were much more valuable.[96] Among the more substantial peasants an increase, rather than a decrease, took place in the number of landholders in the course of the seventeenth century. In the forest of Pendle, Lancashire, for example, the number of medium and small copyholders increased markedly. In four stock-rearing communities in Pendle the fifty-five copyholders in 1608 more than doubled to 129 in 1662.[97] In Nidderdale, Yorkshire, a noticeable decline in the average size of farms had taken place by the late seventeenth century.[98] In Rossendale, Lancashire, seventy-two copyholders in 1507 had increased to 200 by 1608 and to 314 by 1662. The increase was partly brought about by the enclosure of waste land, partly by the subdivision of existing farms. Land was being distributed among more and more people (engrossing was practically unknown), and the process was not reversed in Rossendale even in the eighteenth and nineteenth centuries. After the introduction of cotton manufacture, holdings became more, and not less, minutely subdivided. A rough calculation suggests that the proportion of holdings of less than fifteen acres was two fifths in the seventeenth and two thirds in the nineteenth century.[99]

In other pastoral areas comparisons over time are not possible, but it is clear that at the time of the Parliamentary enclosures many pastoral parishes still had a remarkable number of small proprietors. At Foleshill in Arden, Warwickshire, in 1775, 794 acres were divided between 107 different proprietors. In the fenland of Holland, Lincolnshire, Gosberton had 160 landowners in 1798, Quadring over 150. Small peasants were not noticeably losing their hold on the land, and in some places they were strengthening it in the sense that more people were acquiring a small stake in the soil.[100]

Most writers in the second half of the seventeenth century explicitly or implicitly held the belief that pasture farming was more profitable than corn growing. Charles Davenant, using Gregory King's figures on land use and yields, offered the opinion in 1699 that "it seems more to the national interest of England to employ its land to the breeding and feeding of cattle than to the produce of corn."[101] This general supposition invites belief because it accords with the general trend in agriculture throughout western Europe between 1650 and 1750.[102]

In England pasture farmers enjoyed an assured and relatively stable market for their produce, and solved the problem created by the dwindling size of their holdings by undertaking more industrial employment. These developments caused some writers to press the novel argument that pasture farming supported a larger population than corn. Reckoning in the work created by crops like wool, hemp, and flax, it was plausible. A Gloucestershire agriculturist who had promoted hemp and flax growing argued the case from his own practical experience. He calculated that forty acres of flax would employ more than 800 people for a year, and even allowing a wage bill of 8d. a day for 300 men, 6d. a day for 300 women, and 3d. a day for 200 young people, it would still yield more profit to the sower than 160 acres of corn or grass.[103] Sir Richard Weston claimed that one acre of flax was worth four to five acres of corn; and to prove that pastoral regions generally provided more work than corn lands he turned to the examples of Normandy, Picardy, and Lombardy in France, Holland, Friesland, Zealand, and Flanders—all pastoral regions which, he claimed, were the most populous places in Europe. Dairy farms occupying 100 acres of land employed many more hands than 100 acres of the best corn land; even sheep keeping, while it depopulated the countryside, nevertheless kept a great many people in working the wool into cloth.[104] John Houghton in 1692 argued along the same lines. Did not the wool and skins produced by an acre of pasture create greater employment than tillage? He had made some calculations and promised some time to print them.[105]

While the evidence is circumstantial and fragmentary it seems reasonable to suggest that the pasture-farming regions of the kingdom in the seventeenth century presented a picture of greater economic prosperity for larger numbers of people than the arable regions. The rebuilding of peasant houses in the north and west which took place generally after the Civil War period may perhaps be deemed a further reflection of this prosperity.[106]

The merits of the dual economy of pastoral regions were frequently misunderstood. Defoe gives us one of the few portraits of the farmer-leadminer's life in the Derbyshire Peak. The sight of a family living in a cave with little ready cash filled him with horror. The wife was inordinately grateful when he and his friends tipped the loose change from their purses into her hand. And yet he had to admit that the cave was clean though simple; the children were very bonny, the wife was comely. A close of corn at the door was ready to be harvested. A cow, thin though it was, grazed at hand and pigs rooted about nearby. Bacon hung in the roof. The husband worked in the mines, and when the wife was free, she washed ore.[107] This was clearly a poor family by the standards of pasture-farming communities generally, but it was not the abject hopeless povery of landless, and frequently workless, labourers who formed a growing proportion (at least a third and more) of the population of arable villages in the lowlands.

The most sympathetic and understanding observer of this economy in the later seventeenth century, however, was the Puritan divine, Richard Baxter. Indeed, he is an explicit exponent of the more general argument advanced in the paper. In 1691 he wrote his last treatise, *The Poor Husbandman's Advocate to Rich Racking Landlords.* Baxter came from Kidderminster in Worcestershire, a thickly populated region of peasant workers of every kind, metal workers, nailers, potters, miners, leather workers, and glass workers. He had also lived in and around London, in Westminster, and in Acton, Middlesex. His plea to landlords to show generosity and mercy to husbandmen was not a petition on behalf of all husbandmen, but only on behalf of what he called the racked poor; *not*, he observed, the market gardeners of the Home Counties who, though they paid double the rent for their grounds, had a treble opportunity to improve them. (These are some of our arable farmers producing labour-demanding crops.) "Nor do I speak of those tenants that have some small tenement of £5 or £10 per annum and have besides a trade which doth maintain them." He instanced here weavers, butchers, tailors, joiners, and carpenters. Elsewhere he spoke of the comparative security of life of the nailers, spurriers, swordsmiths, scythesmiths, and sword-makers around Dudley, Stourbridge, Birmingham, Walsall, Wednesbury, and Wolverhamptom. In short, his was an impassioned plea not for peasant-workers in pasture-farming regions, or for arable farmers growing special cash crops, but for the poor husbandmen in the traditional corn-growing districts, whence the small landowners were fast disappearing, and whence, in his view, small tenants were also being driven by rack-renting landlords.[108]

One of the questions that follows from this analysis of social and economic trends in the seventeenth-century countryside is how and why the dual economies in pastoral regions stimulated technical innovation in industry. It is plainly anomalous to expect agricultural innovations of an expensive kind from these regions. The pressure upon industry seems to derive from the very success of the dual economy. As the market for industrial goods expanded, it met labour shortages which peasant-workers could not, or would not, satisfy, and which are reflected in the rapid rise in textile wages in the first half of the eighteenth century.[109] For peasant-workers to turn wholly to industry meant surrendering their hold on the land and surrendering, moreover, a life of varied labour as well as independence.[110] The advantage to the national economy of factory-based industries may seem clear enough if we take a sternly economic view excluding other considerations, but it was purchased at the price of a traditional, and in many respects congenial, life centered upon a smallholding of land, with its industrial annexe. Throughout the seventeenth century, at least, the economics of smallholdings in pastoral regions were not such as to drive the peasant-worker from the land.

Phyllis Deane has recently described in general terms the causes of the industrial and agricultural revolution. She concluded with certain misgivings about generalizations on a national scale. "The national economy is not always the most convenient unit of economic analysis. The effect of regional variations in economic conditions is that statistics relating to a particular area may give no indication of the comparable movements for the nation as a whole, and that the national aggregates may obscure the trends for regions in which the significant changes are taking place. An attempt to assess the quality and rate of economic change at the national level may not lead to meaningful results whether we are looking for the significant continuities or for the significant discontinuities of history."[111] These reflections justify a first attempt at illuminating "the trends for regions in which the significant changes are taking place." It carries the story only to the end of the seventeenth century. To disentangle regional trends from national aggregates, more detailed local studies are needed which will trace developments in the seventeenth century more precisely and, more important, in the early eighteenth century when a further shift of emphasis took place in the economies of both pastoral and arable regions and the ground was finally prepared for two separate revolutions after 1750.

CHAPTER 2

1. W. Notestein, F. H. Relf, and H. Simpson, *Commons Debates, 1621,* 1935, iv, p. 105.

2. Henry Robinson, *Certain Proposals in Order to the People's Freedom and Accommodation,* 1652.

3. *Statutes of the Realm,* v, p. 781.

4. A. H. John, "The Course of Agricultural Change, 1660–1760," in *Studies in the Industrial Revolution,* ed. L. S. Pressnell, 1960, p. 134 *et seq.*; W. G. Hoskins, "Harvest Fluctuations and English Economic History, 1620–1759," *A.H.R.,* xvi, i, 1968, graph facing p. 15. But see also M. Flinn, "Agricultural Productivity and Economic Growth in England, 1700–60: a Comment," *Jnl Econ. Hist.,* xxvi, i, 1966, p. 97, who argues for only a slight secular downward trend in grain prices, 1660–1720.

5. P. J. Bowden, *The Wool Trade in Tudor and Stuart England,* 1962, p.186; Joan Thirsk, *English Peasant Farming,* 1957, p. 193.

6. P.R.O., SP 14/113, no. 21.

7. Bowden, *op. cit.,* pp. 46–8, 213–17, 230; P.R.O., SP 29/176, no. 130; *CSPD 1673–5,* pp. 169–70; Bodleian MS. Top. Kent, A 1, fol. 26; John, *op. cit.,* p. 142.

8. *Ibid.*

9. Notestein, Relf, and Simpson, *op. cit.,* iv, p. 105.

10. P.R.O., SP 29/176, no. 130; Bodleian MS. Top. Kent, A I, fol. 26; Roger Coke, *A Discourse of Trade,* 1670, p. 33; "The Grand Concern of England Explained . . . ," 1673, *Harl. Misc.* 1746, viii, p. 534.

11. John Houghton, *A Collection for the Improvement of Husbandry and Trade,* ed. R. Bradley, 1727, ii, p. 3.

12. Tenants were extremely reluctant to take up land at Ashby de la Zouch, Leics., a grazing parish on the Hastings family estates, in the years 1685–9. I owe this information to the kindness of Mr. Christopher Moxon.

13. Houghton, *op. cit.,* i, pp. 285, 297, 300.

14. Samuel Hartlib, *His Legacie,* 1651, p. 49.

15. P.R.O., SP 16/162, no. 41.

16. Coke, *op. cit.,* p. 34.

17. J. H. Clapham, *A Concise Economic History of Britain,* 1957, p. 285.

18. John, *op. cit.,* p. 144.

19. Houghton, *op. cit.,* i, p. 410.

20. One of the arguments against the Irish Cattle Act was that much pasture had been turned from breeding to dairying purposes before the Irish Cattle Act and such land was now being hit by the competition of Irish butter. I assume that this is a reference to lands in the West Midlands, where there is positive evidence of this change of farming system (see *supra,* pp. 91–2). That Irish butter and cheese were the cause of the low prices of the English product was, however, contested by Houghton. —John Houghton, *A Collection of Letters for the Improvement of Husbandry and Trade,* 1681, i, no. 9, 19 Oct. 1682, p. 87.

21. A more detailed analysis is contained in Joan Thirsk, ed., *The Agrarian History of England and Wales,* IV, *1500–1640,* (henceforth *A.H.E.W.* IV), 1967, pp. 1–112. Cf. also E. L. Jones, *Agriculture and Economic Growth in England, 1650–1815,* 1967, pp. 154 *et seq.*

22. Thirsk, *English Peasant Farming,* p. 192.

23. Michael Havinden, "Agricultural Progress in Open-Field Oxfordshire," *A.H.R.,* ix, ii, 1961, pp. 74–7.

24. Andrew Yarranton, *The Improvement Improved. A Second Edition of the Great Improvement of Lands by Clover,* 1663, pp. 4, 44, 31; P. E. Dove, *Account of Andrew Yarranton. The Founder of English Political Economy,* 1854, p. 8; Bodleian MS. Aubrey 2, fol. 152; G. E. Fussell, "Adventures with Clover," *Agriculture,* lxii, no. 7, 1955, p. 343. The quality of the imported seed in the 1650s was very variable and Walter Blith urged growers to send a reliable man to the Low Countries to buy it, another impracticable suggestion to the small farmer. —W. Blith, *The English Improver Improved,* 1652 edn., p. 179.

25. E. Kerridge, *The Agricultural Revolution,* 1967, pp. 270–6.

26. Thirsk, *A.H.E.W.* IV, p. 168. It is perhaps significant that the early ripening variety of barley used in Oxfordshire which could be sown and returned to the barn in nine or ten weeks—ideal in wet and backward springs—had been introduced to Oxfordshire from Patney in Wiltshire, which was an estate belonging to the Earl of Craven. —R. Plot, *The Natural History of Oxfordshire,* 1676, pp. 152–3; Bodleian MS. Aubrey 2, fol. 84.

27. Royal Society, Georgical Enquiries, Classified Papers, x(3).

28. E. Kerridge, "The Sheepfold in Wiltshire and the Floating of the Water Meadows," *Econ. Hist. Rev.,* 2nd ser., vi, 1954, pp. 286–9; *idem, Agricultural Revolution,* pp. 266–7.

29. E. B. Wood, ed., *Rowland Vaughan, His Booke,* 1897, pp. 30–1.

30. P.R.O., E 178/5669.

31. Kerridge, *Agricultural Revolution,* pp. 254, 262 *et seq.*

32. G. E. Fussell, ed., *Robert Loder's Farm Accounts, 1610–20,* Camden Soc., 3rd ser., liii, 1936; C. B. Robinson, ed., *Rural Economy in Yorkshire in 1641,* Surtees Soc., xxxiii, 1857.

33. Lord Ernle, *English Farming Past and Present,* 1936 edn, pp. 170, 173–4, 218.

34. Thirsk, *English Peasant Farming,* pp. 176–7.

35. Coke, *op. cit.,* p. 15; Bodleian MS. Top. Kent, A1, fol. 26, *Plain English in a*

Familiar Conference betwixt three Friends, Rusticus, Civis, and Veridicus, concerning the Deadness of our Markets, 1673, p. 6.

36. *Considerations concerning Common Fields*, 1654, p. 21.

37. *Leics. V.C.H.*, ii, pp. 204, 223.

38. John Moore, *The Crying Sin of England of not caring for the Poor*, 1653; *idem, A Scripture Word against Inclosure . . .* , 1656; *idem, A Reply to a Pamphlet entitled Considerations . . .* , 1656; *Considerations concerning Common Fields*, 1654; J. Lee, *Vindication of a Regulated Inclosure,* 1656; *A Vindication of the Considerations concerning Common Fields and Inclosures . . .* , 1656. See also W. E. Tate, *The English Village Community . . .* , 1967, p. 77.

39. A. H. Johnson, *The Disappearance of the Small Landowner*, 1963 edn., pp. 132–8.

40. A. C. Chibnall, *Sherington. Fiefs and Fields of a Buckinghamshire Village*, 1965; Margaret Spufford, reviewing the above in *A.H.R.*, 16, i, 1968, p. 72.

41. Margaret Spufford, *A Cambridgeshire Community, Chippenham from Settlement to Enclosure*, Leics. University, Dept. of English Local History, Occasional Paper, no. 20, 1965, pp. 45–6, 48–9. For evidence of the continued decline of the small farmer in the first half of the eighteenth century, see G. E. Mingay "The Size of Farms in the Eighteenth Century," *Econ. Hist. Rev.*, 2nd ser., xiv, 1962, pp. 481–4. Cf. also the statement of William Ellis that it is doubtful "whether since the early part of the eighteenth century it has profited the man of middle acres to own the land he farms." Cited in Charles Wilson, *England's Apprenticeship*, 1965, p. 252. See also H. J. Habakkuk, "La Disparition du paysan anglais," *Annales E.S.C.*, 20e annee, 1965, no. 4, pp. 649–63.

42. Culpeper, Preface to the 1st edn., 1668; Carew Reynel, *The True English Interest*, 1674, p. 20.

43. H. C. Pawson, *Robert Bakewell*, 1957, pp. 18 *et seq;* D. J. Rowe, "The Culleys—Northumberland Farmers, 1767–1813," forthcoming article in the *A.H.R.*

44. W. G. Hoskins, *The Midland Peasant*, 1957, pp. 97–110, 228.

45. Mea Allen, *The Tradescants, their Plants, Gardens, and Museum, 1570–1663, 1964, passim.* See also *infra*, p. 160.

46. Thomas Mun, *England's Treasure by Foreign Trade* in J. R. McCulloch, *Early English Tracts on Commerce*, 1952, pp. 115 *et seq.* It was published in 1664 but was written in 1623. —B. Supple, "Thomas Mun and the Commercial Crisis, 1623," *B.I.H.R.*, xxvii, 1954, pp. 91–4.

47. Some of the same ideas occur in the earlier pamphlets by Henry Robinson, namely, *England's Safety in Trade's Increase*, 1641, and *Brief Considerations concerning the Advancement of Trade and Navigation*, 1649. See also William Goffe, "How to Advance the Trade of the Nation and Employ the Poor," *Harl. Misc.* iv, pp. 385–9.

48. Sir William Coventry, "Essay concerning the Decay of Rents and their Remedies," 1670, Brit. Mus., Sloane MS. 3828, fols. 205–10. See also "The Grand Concern of England explained," 1673, *Harl. Misc.*, viii, 1746, p. 544, referring to the "leaving off eating of suppers."

49. Ronald Webber, *The Early Horticulturists*, 1968, p. 41.

50. Walter Blith, *The English Improver, or a New Survey of Husbandry,* 1649, title page; *idem, The English Improver Improved,* 1652, pp. 224–5.

51. Kerridge, *Agricultural Revolution,* 1967, pp. 194, 210–11.

52. Philip Miller, *The Method of Cultivating Madder,* 1758, *passim;* J. Mortimer, *The Whole Art of Husbandry,* 1707, pp. 123 *et seq.;* Blith, 1653 edn., *op. cit.,* p. 235.

53. P.R.O., SP 16/164, nos. 53 & 53, i-iii; L. B. Larking, *Proceedings principally in the Country of Kent . . . ,* Camden Soc., 1862, pp. 54–5.

54. Blith, 1652, *op. cit.,* p. 235; Houghton, ed. Bradley, *op. cit.,* ii, p. 372.

55. W. Coles, *Adam in Eden,* 1657, pp. 584–5; Blith, 1652, *op. cit.,* p. 233.

56. P.R.O., SP 14/113, no. 21; Blith, 1652, *op. cit.,* pp. 226–7, 230; L. Meager, *The Mystery of Husbandry . . .,* 1697, p. 106; Guildford Muniment Room, Loseley MS., 1965; 1966, 1–4; Hants. Country Record Office, 1583, B. I owe this reference to Miss Adrienne Batchelor.

57. John Banister, *Synopsis of Husbandry,* 1799, pp. 197–202. This is the most circumstantial account of weld growing known to me. I wish to thank Mr. Dennis Baker for the reference. See also Blith, 1652, *op. cit.,* pp. 222–5; Houghton, ed. Bradley, *op. cit.,* ii, p. 459; Mortimer, *op. cit.,* p. 127.

58. Houghton, ed. Bradley, *op. cit.,* iii, pp. 354–5; iv, p. 361; Hist. MSS. Comm., ix, *House of Lords MSS.,* p. 28; Carew Reynel, *op. cit.,* p. 87. A petition against a duty on safflower *c.* 1670 says that not more than 2,000 lb. were then grown in England compared with 600 cwt which was imported from Germany. This was in the early days of its commercial cultivation in England. —*CSPD 1660–85, Addenda,* p. 505.

59. W. Coles, *The Art of Simpling,* 1656, p. 51; *idem, Adam in Eden,* p. 172; Houghton, ed. Bradley, *op. cit.,* ii, pp. 331–2; iv, pp. 283–7; Blith, 1652, *op. cit.,* p. 244; Mortimer, *op. cit.,* pp. 129–30.

60. Blith, 1652, *op. cit.,* pp. 246–8; Houghton, ed. Bradley, *op. cit.,* iv, pp. 41–3; Mortimer *op. cit.,* pp. 127–9; John Parkinson, *Paradisi in Sole,* 1656, p. 472.

61. P.R.O., SP 46/100, fol. 242, lists an order for vegetable seeds, 1656(?); 1¹/₂ lb. of best onion seed cost 5s., ¹/₂ lb. lettuce seed 2s., and ¹/₄ peck of radish seed 2s.

62. The Venetian Busoni said that gravelly land around London was dug out to about six-seven feet and filled up with the filth of the city, so making it very fertile for garden crops. —Webber, *op. cit.,* p. 51; Mortimer, *op. cit.,* p. 146.

63. John Houghton, *England's Great Happiness or a Dialogue between Content and Complaint,* 1677, p. 12; Blith, 1652, *op. cit.,* p. 261; *Philos. Trans.* x-xii, no. 116, p. 363.

64. *Philos. Trans.,* x-xii, no. 131, p. 796; no. 136, p. 922; Hist. MSS. Comm., *Portland II,* p. 30; P.R.O., E 134, 33 & 34 Chas. II, Hil. 26; 13 & 14 Chas. II, Hil. 7; 21 Chas. II, Trin. 7; 3 Jas. II, Easter 2.

65. See bibliography in Webber, *op. cit.; Philos. Trans.,* x-xii, pp. 303, 373–4, 922.

66. Middlesex County Record Office, M1, 1718/10; 1684/93; 1686/36; 1682/18.

67. Gregory King's estimates do not help us to make any very accurate guesses. He estimated the value of hemp, flax, woad, saffron, and dyes at £1,000,000, and the produce of arable land (grains and legumes) at £10,000,000. But hemp and flax are treated in my analysis as the products of pastoral regions, and King omitted

vegetables entirely. —George E. Barnett, ed., *Two Tracts by Gregory King*, 1936, p. 36.

68. Brit. Mus., Sloan MS. 3828, fols. 205–10.

69. The value of these crops in relieving poverty among the increasing population of the Netherlands is discussed in B. H. Slicher van Bath, "Historical Demography and the Social and Economic Development of the Netherlands," *Daedalus*, Spring 1968, pp. 612, 614.

70. P.R.O., E 134, 14 Chas. I, Mich. 31; SP 25, 1, 75, pp. 374–5, 409; SP 18, 72, no. 65; R. Steele, *A Bibliography of Royal Proclamation of the Tudor and Stuart Sovereigns*, p. 150, 30 Dec. 1619, gives the first proclamation banning tobacco growing throughout England and Wales.

71. Hist. MSS. Comm., *Portland II*, p. 303.

72. A good example of a corn-growing village which was converted to pasture is the Verney family's home at Claydon, Bucks. It was a "closed" village in which the rich farmers were graziers and the poor were dairymen. The surplus population which could not find work in the parish or in neighbouring ones drifted to London. I wish to thank Mr. John Broad for this information.

73. Brit. Mus., Thomason Tracts, E 669 f15(21) and (23); Keith Thomas, "Another Digger Broadside," *Past and Present*, 42, 1969, pp. 57–68.

74. These farming types are mapped in Thirsk, *A.H.E.W.* iv, p. 4.

75. Joan Thirsk, "Horn and Thorn in Staffordshire. The Economy of a Pastoral County," *North Staffs. Jnl. of Field Studies*, 9, 1969, pp. 3–4.

76. H. C. Darby, *The Draining of the Fens*, 2nd edn., 1968, pp. 49–58; P.R.O., SP 16, 185, no. 2; Acts of the Privy Council, 1630–31, nos. 329, 330, 536, 646, 816, 818, 835, 855, 1041, 1057, 1129, 1130, 1156, 1158, 1165. See also E. Kerridge, "The Revolts in Wiltshire against Charles I," *Wilts. Arch. and Nat. Hist. Mag.* lvii, 1958-9, pp. 64-75.

77. For three examples of reports and tracts on this subject, see SP 18/69, no. 6 ("Proposals by Dr. John Parker and Edward Cressett for best Improvement of the Forests," 1654): Silvanus Taylor, *Common Good or the Improvement of Commons, Forests, and Chases . . .* , 1652; Appendix to Blith, 1652, *op. cit.*, pp. 263 *et seq.*, entitled "A Remonstrance . . . for regulating forests, Wastes, or Commons . . ."

78. J. Houghton, *A Collection for Improvement of Husbandry and Trade*, 1692, p. 76.

79. Thirsk, *English Peasant Farming*, pp. 126–7.

80. P.R.O., SP 46/88, fols. *et seq.*, illustrate the experiences of Rumbold Jacobson, merchant of London and lessee of 428 acres of Hatfield Chase, *c.* 1640-1. The report in 1654 by Parker and Cressett (see above, p. 101, n. 77), discussing the possibility of improving the forests by leasing out large portions, assumed that the commoners would not take up such leases out of hostility to the whole project, while "others will be very tender of disgusting their neighbours the commoners in hiring it from them" —P.R.O., SP 18, 69, no. 6.

81. See *supra* pp. 74–75.

82. Royal Society, Georgical Enquiries, Classified Papers, x(3) *passim*. These reports are summarized in R. V. Lennard, "English Agriculture under Charles II . . . ," *Econ. Hist. Rev.*, IV, 1932–4, pp. 23–45; Blith, 1652, *op. cit.*, p. 38, my italics.

83. Samuel Hartlib, *His Legacie*, 1651, p. 96. These remarks were made with particular reference to dairy cattle.

84. Bernard Jennings, ed., *A History of Nidderdale*, 1967, pp. 171–2, 176.

85. P. E. Dove, *Account of Andrew Yarranton, the Founder of English Political Economy*, 1854, p. 44.

86. Blith, 1652, *op. cit.*, p. 254.

87. Robert Sharrock, *An Improvement to the Art of Gardening*, 1694, pp. 43–4. The evidence for larger crops of hemp and flax comes from the glebe terriers of Staffordshire which refer with increasing frequency, 1698–1735, to tithes of hemp and flax in the parishes of the county. I wish to thank Mr. B. B. Evans for assembling this evidence for me and allowing me to use it here.

88. Blith, 1652, *op. cit.*, pp. 251, 254; Michael Williams, "The Draining and Reclamation of Meare Pool, Somerset," Thirteenth Annual Report, Somerset River Board, 1962–3, Bridgwater, 1963, p. 1; Thirsk, *A.H.E.W.* iv, p. 13; Richard Weston, *Discourse of Husbandry used in Brabant and Flanders*, 2nd edn, ed. Samuel Hartlib, 1652, p. 18.

89. Hartlib, *His Legacie*, pp. 40–1; Houghton, ed. Bradley, *op. cit.*, ii, p. 389.

90. Cf. Marie B. Rowlands, "Industry and Social Change in Staffordshire, 1660–1760," *Trans. Lichfield & S. Staffs. Arch. & Hist. Soc.*, ix, 1967–8, p. 39.

91. Quoted by Edward Thompson in "Time, Work-Discipline, and Industrial Capitalism," *Past and Present*, 38, pp. 71–2.

92. They represented 11.2 percent of the total number of occupiers of land in England and Wales in the National Farm Survey of 1941–3.

93. Wladislaw Adamski, "Investigations on Off-Farm Income in Poland," summary of a paper read to a seminar at Birmingham University on Peasant Farming in Europe, March 1968.

94. Thirsk, *A.H.E.W.* iv, pp. 409–12; Coke, *op. cit.*, p. 16.

95. Thirsk, *English Peasant Farming*, pp. 141, 168–70; J. M. Martin, "The Parliamentary Enclosure Movement and Rural Society in Warwickshire," *A.H.R.*, xv, i, p. 20.

96. Thirsk, *A.H.E.W.* iv, pp. 400–6.

97. Mary Brigg, "The Forest of Pendle in the Seventeenth Century," *Trans. Lancs. and Cheshire Hist. Soc.*, cxiii, 1961, p. 72.

98. Jennings, ed., *op. cit.*, pp. 147, 171–2.

99. G. H. Tupling, *The Economic History of Rossendale*, Chetham Soc., n.s., 86, 1927, pp. 76, 235, 95, 227–9.

100. J. M. Martin, "Warwickshire and the Parliamentary Enclosure Movement," Birmingham University Ph.D. thesis, 1965, pp. 80–1; David Grigg, *The Agricultural Revolution in South Lincolnshire,* 1966, p. 84. Cf. the saying that the Isle of Axholme had so many freeholders that whoever got the Isle could get the county. —Francis Hill, *Georgian Lincoln*, p. 30.

101. Charles Davenant, *An Essay upon the Probable Methods of Making a People Gainers in the Balance of Trade*, 1699, pp. 88–9.

102. B. H. Slicher van Bath, *The Agrarian History of Western Europe, A.D. 500–1850*, 1963, pp. 206–17.

103. P.R.O., SP 14/180, no. 79.

104. Hartlib, *His Legacie,* pp. 55–6. Hartlib listed the commodites got from cattle (meaning cattle and sheep) as cloth, stuffs, stockings, butter, cheese, hides, shoes, and tallow.

105. Houghton, ed. Bradley, *op. cit.,* I, p. 49.

106. M. W. Barley, *The English Farmhouse and Cottage,* 1961, pp. 227, 230, 236, 244.

107. D. Defoe, *A Tour through England and Wales,* Everyman edn., II, pp. 161–3.

108. F. J. Powicke, ed., *The Reverend Richard Baxter's Last Treatise,* John Rylands Library Publication, 1926, pp. 25–8.

109. Professor Crouzet suggests in a recent essay that one of the two most powerful stimuli to technical innovation was the shortage of labour in the handicraft industries of S. Lancs., Yorks., the Midlands, and in the metal-working industries of the Black Country. —F. Crouzet, "Angleterre et France au XVIIIe siècle. Essai d'analyse comparée de deux croissances économiques," *Annales E.S.C.,* 21e année, no. 2, 1966, pp. 286–7. See also E. W. Gilboy, *Wages in Eighteenth-Century England,* 1934, p. 191 *et seq.*

110. This is the view of Gilboy, *op. cit.,* p. 143, and is supported by other authorities there cited. See also Crouzet, *op. cit.,* p. 288; N. J. Smelser, *Social Change in the Industrial Revolution,* 1959, p. 77.

111. Phyllis Deane, *The First Industrial Revolution,* 1965, pp. 17–18.

Professor Coleman in the present article examines a major reason for the failure of that radical change to occur in seventeenth-century England. As he notes, Englishmen at the time assumed that most of the labouring population were poor and would remain so, although most hoped that the numerous poor would on the whole be gainfully employed. And as he notes also, such attitudes were not so much the product of brutally insensitive exploiters as a reflection of an economy characterized by low wages, seasonal unemployment, and widespread under-employment. An industrial revolution would have altered these conditions, but low wages and under-employment prevented the development of a mass consumption market that was necessary to sustained growth.

D. C. Coleman is a Fellow of Pembroke College and Professor of Economic History at Cambridge. Two of his interests —in mercantilism and in the process of industrialization—come together in the present article, and his continued preoccupation with the former theme can be seen in Revisions in Mercantilism *(London, 1969), which he edited and introduced. He is also the author of a history of* The British Paper Industry, 1495–1860 *(Oxford, 1958), a biography of the seventeenth-century financier* Sir John Banks: Baronet and Businessman *(Oxford, 1963), and* Courtaulds: An Economic and Social History, 2 vols. *(Oxford, 1969). The present article first appeared in the* Economic History Review, *2nd series, 8 (1956), 280–95, and is reprinted by permission of the author and the journal.*

Labour in the English Economy of the Seventeenth Century[1]

D. C. Coleman

I

Seventeenth-century writers were in fairly general agreement about "the labouring poor." Three particular points of agreement may be distinguished. First, they knew that there were many of them and in the course of the century they came to believe that there should be still more. Second, they were at pains to insist that this large labouring population which they desired should always be kept adequately and properly employed. And third, this attitude was usually paralleled by the firm belief that the poor should remain poor.

Even if no seventeenth-century writer quite achieved the resounding simplicity of Arthur Young's famous utterance on this last point[2] or even of Mandeville's variations on this theme,[3] such Stuart authors as Thomas Mun and Sir William Temple explicitly linked penury and want with wisdom and hard work; and Peter Chamberlen, writing in 1649, contended that "the poor" could be "the richest treasure of a nation, if orderly and well employed."[4]

Although some writers in the earlier years of the century contended that the country had too many people (see below, p. 129), the desirability of a larger population was voiced firmly and frequently after the mid-century. A clear expression of this view was given by Charles Davenant, who, holding that the people were "the first matter of power and wealth," was amongst those who advocated a policy of the deliberate stimulation of increase.[5] Though others were less explicit, such writers as Child, Petty, Pollexfen, and the author of *Brittania Languens* all put forward similar views, variously linking large numbers with lower wages, lower prices, and, at the same time, with prosperity. As Pollexfen put it, "The more are maintained by Laborious Profitable Trades, the richer the Nation will be both in People and Stock and . . . Commodities the cheaper."[6]

The necessity to "employ the poor" is a theme which is reiterated time and time again in this period, enlivened by frequent blasts against "idleness." To the statements of writers and pamphleteers there can be added the preambles of a long series of Acts of Parliament, the utterances and writings of statesmen, the reports of public bodies. Continually recurring in Tudor and Stuart legislation about trade and industry is the familiar clause claiming that such and such an industry employs so many thousand men, women, and children—usually a figure of suspicious roundness and improbable magnitude. Individual industries and particular branches of commerce were judged by their ability to absorb labour or stimulate employment. This determination to employ took the form of advocating various "make-work" projects and produced opposition, amongst the more conservative writers, to labour-saving devices even in agriculture: "that being the best way of tillage which employeth most about it, to keep them from stealing and starving."[7]

The desirability of keeping down wages did not achieve quite so impressive a show of unanimity, though on the whole both the views of writers and the tenor of policy clearly pointed in this direction. John Cary was well in advance of the prevailing ideas of his time when, in 1695, he linked the virtues of technical innovations and labour-saving devices with the merits of high wages; and so was Dudley North, who wrote in similar terms in 1701;[8] Defoe plainly advocated the economy of high wages. But these ideas were certainly exceptional. Large numbers and low wages was a link commonly made. Child observed that "the riches of a city as of a nation consist in the multitudes of inhabitants,"[9] and elsewhere produced the customary corollary that "much want of people would procure greater wages"; the author of *Brittania Languens* provided the straightforward statement that "The odds in Populacy must also produce the like odds in Manufacture: plenty of people must also cause cheapnesse of wages: which will cause the cheapnesse of the Manufacture."[10] And, of course, the main purpose of wage-fixing policy was to assess maximum and not minimum wages. Though there was one important exception to this, though wages were paid which were higher than the assessed rates, though the "labouring poor" periodically appealed against the paucity of their rewards, in spite of all this there seems little reason to quarrel with Heckscher's judgement that "the State everywhere exerted its influence on the side of low wages."[11]

II

How have historians attempted to explain or assess these attitudes? In what economic context have they been seen?

The main avenues of approach to the subject have been those which lead to the study of social policy, particularly the Poor Law, and, above all, that broad and comprehensive highway labelled "mercantilism." This has led, on the one hand, to what are essentially studies in administrative history which rarely ask economic questions; and on the other hand, to the pursuit of a nebulous entity. The longer the chase, the larger and more indefinable has this so-called entity grown. The concept of "mercantilism," of a "mercantile system," inflated into something larger and more engulfing than Adam Smith envisaged, has certainly been the justification for some remarkable books (one thinks of Heckscher's monumental study), but it has inhibited the asking of fundamental economic questions about the nature of economies in which certain characteristics of policy appeared. The notion of "mercantilism" has come to dictate both the questions which are asked and the answers which are found. Heckscher's great work opens with the words "Mercantilism never existed in the sense that Colbert or Cromwell existed." A salutary warning, for by the time the reader has reached the end of the second volume, it has become evident that something akin to an act of creation has taken place. "Mercantilism," he continued, is "an instrumental concept which . . . should enable us to understand a particular historical period more clearly than we otherwise might."[12] He has much to say on the subject of labour, but when finally he comes to assess or explain the attitudes to labour in this period, to place them in their economic and social context, he writes simply that the attitude towards labour "was bound up with the idea of a suitable subsistence and the inferiority of the masses to the privileged classes—both medieval ideas"; or again, "Mercantilism inherited from the past the tendency towards low wages and abundant supply in the labour market."[13] Will economic historians of some future century, if any there be, fasten on to our own time some such tag as "The Age of Keynesianism" and then inquire into our economy from that vantage point?

Even Edgar Furniss's brilliant essay *The Position of the Labourer in a System of Nationalism* succumbs to the power which the study of "mercantilism" seems to wield, the power to beget assumptions which, in other contexts, would seem unreasonable and which hinder the asking of economic questions. His basic assumption is that the "mercantilist" writers were overwhelmingly concerned with the need for state power via the favourable balance of trade and from this position he then makes his inquiry into the attitudes which both the writers and the State were forced to adopt towards the labourer. In a recent article on this subject[14] another writer has contended that "full employment was *the* economic objective of mercantilist polity" (my italics).

That both writers and the State were concerned, *inter alia*, with employment and that there was a striking similarity in their opinions is true enough. But this is not the same as assuming that there was something called "mercantile policy" which was peculiarly concerned with "full employment." And more important is the question: why, amongst all their other concerns and agreements, should there have been this interest in and unanimity about idleness, employment, and labour? To this question answers are few and far between.[15] The existence of unemployment is ascribed mainly to commercial crises and the enclosure movement; it is agreed that poverty was common; some attention is paid, especially by Furniss and Heckscher, to the relationship between wages and labour supply. Is this adequate to explain a concern with labour and employment which showed remarkable unanimity over a long period? What is the nature of the unemployment or the poverty which should thus cause such a consistency in attitude? What, in brief, was the position of labour in the working of the economy?

III

Any attempt to answer these questions and to see the reasons for the attitude alike of the State and of the writers must start with an examination of the nature of the economy. As a crude, first approximation it may be suggested that the answers must be sought, first, in the long-term forces which made up the economic bases of the society of the time; and, second, in the short- and medium-term developments or extraneous pressures which fashioned the nature or determined the timing of particular events or attitudes.[16]

Before examining these, however, it will be useful first to review the evidence of the numbers of the working class and the proportion which they bore to the rest of the community.

If the economists and social pamphleteers wanted a larger body of labouring poor, there is no lack of evidence that in mere numbers the poor already formed a very substantial part of the total population. Contemporary comment upon the numbers of poor stretches back into the sixteenth century, at least, and forward into the eighteenth. To Bacon, labourers and cottagers were "but house beggars"; to a writer of the 1640s it seemed reasonable to suppose that "the fourth part of the inhabitants of most of the parishes of England are miserable poor people, and (harvest time excepted) without any subsistence."[17] The comprehensive and well-known investigations of Gregory King in the 1680s and 1690s tell an even grimmer tale. He classes 23 percent of the national population as "labouring people and out servants" and a further 24 percent as "cottagers and paupers," estimating that both groups had annual family expenditures greater than income.[18]

How acceptable are King's estimates and how far are they true of other times in this period? His calculations of total population have been shown by Professor Glass to be reasonably reliable.[19] Modern inquiries in local history, notably those of Dr. Hoskins, have helped to confirm the accuracy of King's use of the Hearth Tax data and also the general feasibility of his estimates; in Tudor Leicester, for example, "fully one-half of the population lived below or very near the poverty line."[20] King's estimates and all others based on tax returns are admittedly open to the objection that they may merely reflect the success of those who contrived, on plea of poverty, to avoid payment of tax. I am inclined, nevertheless, to accept the general magnitude suggested by King's figures, though with certain qualifications which will become apparent later. In the light of the high and increasing figures at which the cost of poor relief was put, especially after the Restoration, in the light of the continually reiterated complaints about the burden of poverty,[21] such percentages are not inherently improbable. As Mrs. George has remarked, "perhaps the most startling thing about [King's estimates] is that to his contemporaries there was nothing surprising in his figures."[22]

This, then, may be taken as a starting point: that in Stuart England between a quarter and a half of the entire population were chronically below what contemporaries regarded as the official poverty line. Skilled artisans as well as those who came within the comprehensive embrace of the term "yeomen" were outside this group. But it undoubtedly included the majority of both unskilled and semi-skilled working class: cottagers and labourers, agricultural and industrial, the poor weaver as well as the poor husbandman, so lamented by Richard Baxter.[23]

IV

What was the nature of the economy in which this situation existed? The first and obvious point of departure in answering this question is to stress that we are dealing with the pre-industrialized, pre-mechanized, predominantly agricultural economy. It is of the type which is today called backward or, more politely, underdeveloped. It is to economies of this sort that we should look in order to see the reflexions of many, though obviously not all, of the economic features of seventeenth-century England.

We can see some of these features reflected as soon as we begin to ask, for example, demographic questions. Particularly relevant in the present context is the age-structure of the population. The first immediately apparent point here is that both in the England of the seventeenth century and in the backward society of today, a much larger proportion of the population is composed of children than in the modern industrialized or otherwise economically advanced community. The following examples may serve to illustrate this:

PERCENTAGES OF POPULATION UNDER 15[24]

(i)

England and Wales	1695	38.4
Sweden	1750	33.3
Finland	1751	38.2
England and Wales	1821	39.1

(ii)

India	1951	38.3
Algeria *(Moslem Population)*	1953	42.5
Ecuador	1950	42.5
South Korea	1952	41.1
Malaya	1947	39.9
Egypt	1937	39.2

(iii)

England	1951	22.3
U.S.A.	1952	28.3
Belgium	1951	21.1
West Germany	1950	23.6
Sweden	1948	22.6
France	1950	21.7

These figures suggest that, in the economies of the so-called mercantilist era, the proportion of the young in the population was only a little less than in the backward communities of the present day, a similarity carrying with it similar social problems.[25]

This state of affairs must now be considered in conjunction with the fact that, in seventeenth-century England, average expectation of life at birth was probably in the neighborhood of thirty-five or less.[26] A further item of information which one would like to know is the average length of working life in the seventeenth century. This we do not know. Some persons undoubtedly lived to considerable ages; indeed, it is likely that once a man or a woman had successfully overcome the hazards of life in early years, there was a reasonable chance of surviving to a mature old age. But at what age most people became a drag on the community in the sense that the incapacity of age either rendered them unfit for work or, at any rate, substantially lowered their productive efficiency is another matter. A rough comparison with modern England may be made either by comparing the percentages of the population falling within the age bracket of, say, fifteen to sixty, or by comparing the percentages between fifteen and the expectation of life figure. By the former method, these groups comprised 51 percent of the population in 1695, and in 1951 nearly 66 percent; by the latter method, in 1695 the groups from fifteen to thirty-five covered 31 percent, in 1951 from fifteen to the male expectation of life figure of sixty-five they accounted for nearly 67 percent.[27] It may reasonably be assumed, therefore, that in seventeenth-century England the labour force of the community was characterized by a relatively short span of working life at maximum productive efficiency; by the need to support a comparatively large body of children who, though certainly not unproductive in those days, may be presumed to have had a relatively low productive efficiency; and finally by the probable need also to support many at the other end of the scale, those whose efficient working life was over.

These demographic conditions were an important aspect of the high incidence of poverty amongst the working classes of Stuart England. This can be brought out more clearly by examining the relationship between pauperism, family size, and age as shown in an enumeration of the population of Lichfield in 1695.[28] In this census, which was one of the sources from which Gregory King made his estimate of the age-structure of the national population, a number of persons are described as "paupers." The accuracy of this classification is not known, but it seems reasonable to regard it as a minimum rather than a maximum. Those labelled as paupers formed only 5.3 percent of the total population of the town; but about half were men and women between the ages of thirty and fifty, of whom most were heads of families. In order, therefore, to get a better idea of what may be called the "pauperized" section of this particular town, it is necessary to include the wives and children, not themselves described as paupers, of heads of families who were described as paupers. Add to this a small number of persons described as "almswomen" and/or "hospitall men" and "hospitall women," nearly all of whom were very old, and we may have a rough idea of those directly and indirectly in the pauperized category. This group forms 16.8 percent of the population of the time. At first glance this seems low compared with King's general estimate, but it must be remembered that this almost certainly only covers those who were directly or indirectly dependent upon relief at that time. It takes no account of those who were adjudged too poor to pay various taxes: it corresponds, roughly, with only the "pauper" part of King's large group of "cottagers and paupers."

If this 16.8 percent is now broken down into age groups we find that the children under fifteen form 47.3 percent of the pauperized group, compared with 37.1 percent of the total town population. To put it another way: of all the children under fifteen in the town, 23.8 percent came from families where the head of the family was described as pauper. Similarly, at the other end of the scale, nearly 17 percent of the pauperized were sixty years of age and over, compared with rather less than 6 percent of the total population.[29]

Could the data be traced and analyzed, it might well be found that such a situation as this was typical of the country as a whole, though there is one difference in the situation as between rural areas and large towns which may be noted at this point. In the bigger towns the percentage under fifteen would normally be smaller than in the countryside because of rural-urban migration by young adults.[30] Hence, it is likely that the problem of dependent children formed a relatively more important source of poverty amongst the rural labouring families than amongst urban. There is one estimate of King's which hints at the general picture. His calculations based on the Poll Tax of 1691[31] classify 55 percent of the national population as "excused or insolvent." This 55 percent was made up, approximately, thus: those receiving alms and those not paying to the Church and Poor Rates together accounted for 24 percent; most of the remaining 31 percent was composed of the children under sixteen of these two groups and of certain others of the lowest social strata. In particular, it is worth noting that those receiving alms and their children under sixteen together accounted for 17.3 percent, which corresponds very closely with the 16.8 percent of the pauperized group in Lichfield. Poverty amongst the "labouring poor" was, in part at least, a problem of supporting the young and of caring for the old as, of course, it very often is today. King's commonly used Hearth Tax estimates need to be interpreted in conjunction with his (and others) less commonly used calculations relating to family size, age, and life expectation.

In such circumstances, child labour is surely normal. If children were not put to useful employment then, as Yarranton said in the 1670s, "he that has most is poorest."[32] The enthusiastic desire voiced by various English (and French) commentators to see all the children of the poor vigorously employed,[33] or the often-quoted raptures of Defoe on observing this during his "Tour" spring from an awareness, however crude, of basic demographic circumstances and owe less than is sometimes suggested to Puritan doctrine or to nationalist fervour. Similarly, the frequent appearances on the social scene, in these earlier centuries, of the orphan or the parish child needs to be seen against this demographic background, just as does our concern with the old today.

These demographic conditions were themselves partly a reflection of another general feature of the economy: all forms of activity were far more subject than in the industrialized economy of today to the interference of natural phenomena. This is another way, of course, of emphasizing that we are dealing with an economy virtually unaffected by the changes brought by scientific achievement. It is just this which makes the age-structure and life expectation of the backward economy "natural" or "normal." Those of the modern advanced society are, in a similar sense, man-made. In the seventeenth century nature left its mark in innumerable ways, be it through the ravages of disease on man, beasts, and crops alike or through the tyranny of the seasons, limiting man's work in agriculture, fishing, and industry, by day and by night, by winter and by summer, according to the vagaries of the weather. All this is well enough known, but perhaps insufficiently heeded, by the economic historian, who too often ascribes to state policy or to short-term forces a potency which neither possesses; this sometimes helps to obscure the essentially primitive elements in the economy.

In this economy, continually at the mercy of natural forces, and having the demographic conditions just outlined, labour was easily the most important factor of production. When Davenant wrote simply that "the bodies of men are without doubt the most valuable treasure of a country,"[34] he was not revealing some recondite economic truth, nor was he saying something which demands explanation in terms of the continuity of a certain line of economic thought. He was stating something obvious to any contemporary who bothered to observe and think about the economy of his day and age, just as obvious and as natural as the long perceived and crude form of labour theory of value. Not only in food production, but in the all-important cloth industry, labour was the most important item in direct production costs. Only in a small number of industries using more or less heavy fixed capital equipment, such as iron smelting or paper-making, did such other items as fuel or raw materials take precedence over labour.

Furthermore, the continuing backwardness of techniques meant not only that productivity per worker was low, but that the chances of increasing it by means of capital investment in labour-saving, and thus cost-reducing, devices were slender: even had there been the capital available, the scope for its application was slight. The labour-saving or productivity-increasing devices which were in use at the time were often centuries old: the fulling mill, the spinning wheel, the enclosed and consolidated farm, the water-powered blast furnace; others were just making their appearance at the end of the century. Low productivity, static techniques, and labour as the main factor of production meant long hours of arduous toil to produce a small amount. Consequently, in order to raise total output, a wish often expressed by later Stuart writers, it was necessary to increase the number of producing units. Qualitative improvement being virtually impossible, quantitative increases had to suffice. This in turn gave to natural increase of population an especial importance and thus provided a comprehensible economic basis upon which was erected the advocacy of a large population, at the same time allowing writers very reasonably to point to the comparative poverty of sparsely populated countries.

As the England of the time was an economy with a low national income and output and low personal incomes for all but a very few, there was, for most of the people most of the time, little or nothing left for savings, and opportunities for consumption were severely restricted. The overwhelming bulk of the income of ordinary persons was spent on necessities of life and on a very small range of conventional consumer goods. Such circumstances as these lay behind the prevailing conception of the inelasticity of demand, of a limited and not readily expandable economic horizon, so often encountered in the utterances and attitudes of the day.

*   *   *

The interaction of these long-term forces sets up tensions, creates other pressures within the structure of the economy. These, to change the metaphor, form a pattern which makes up the background to the whole picture of the seventeenth-century English economy. The particular age-structure and expectation of life of the population kept low the numbers of the working force at the ages of maximum efficiency; the continuing expansion of the economy in trade, industry, and agriculture, together with the vital importance of labour as a factor of production and the slow rate of population growth, increased the demand for labour. Thus there was generated a pressure tending to push up wages. But just as such circumstances provided the vital reasons for child labour, so they did also for the continuing policies of wage restraint. In the same way, the interaction of the long-term forces also lies at the bottom of another of the Stuart obsessions: the problem of employment. It does so because these various essential elements of the economy combined to produce a persistent tendency towards chronic under-employment.

This is a characteristic of the modern backward economy which has achieved some recognition in comparatively recent years. It has been seen as something different from the cyclical or frictional unemployment recurrently marking industrialized communities. Professor Tawney commented in the 1930s that in some areas of China only about 100 days per year were spent on farm employments and that, for many of the unskilled urban workers, half-employment was the rule, "so that employed and unemployed melt into each other." It is not a spectre which haunts Asiatic countries alone; the problems of under-employment have been observed in communities as distant and as superficially diverse as, take but two examples, British Guiana on one side of the Atlantic and southern Italy on the other. It was said recently that the average agricultural labourer of southern Italy is lucky if he finds 180 days' work in a year, an estimate remarkably similar to the results of comparable calculations relating to various parts of Asia; not more than 150 days' full labour per year was given as the figure for the average cultivator of the Punjab, for example.[35]

Under-employment may, broadly speaking, be visible or concealed. Visible under-employment can roughly be defined as the difference between the amount of working time which the labour force could theoretically supply and that which it in fact does contribute to the economy *in the existing methods of production.* Concealed under-employment need not be considered here, for it rests upon the possibility of changes in the methods of production. In one form or another it stems essentially from low productivity; it is normally treated today by heavy doses of the favourite modern medicine, the substitution of capital for labour, on a scale unknown to the seventeenth century.

Visible under-employment, on the other hand, was visible to contemporaries, and it was largely this which lay behind the constant reiteration of the well-worn theme about employing the poor. It arose first in this predominantly food-producing economy from the nature of labour demand in farming. Methods of cultivation, the lay-out of farms, the size of holdings, the comparatively limited range of crops in general cultivation—these doubtless led to under-employment in all its forms. But the obvious source of it was the seasonality of work in backward agriculture, the inability of this form of productive activity to provide constant or continuous employment, "full employment" in a particular sense of the phrase, though *not* the Keynesian sense.

In a work published in 1705, John Law, developing an argument about the role of money in the economy, reasoned from an imaginary "Crusoe" economy. He supposed the existence of an island owned by one man and populated by tenant farmers, with their families, 1,000 in all, who laboured partly at grain production and partly at pasturage. In addition, it is interesting to note, he assumed the existence of "300 Poor and Idle who live by Charity." The society did not use money, rents being paid in kind; it produced a surplus of agricultural products which it traded overseas for clothing, etc. Law then imagined the introduction of money and the setting up of manufactures in the island in order to make the goods which had been imported. In developing his argument he makes two most significant remarks. He said that in this way the poor might be employed. Further, he said that *"as the 1000 that labour the Ground were idle one half of their time,* they might be employed so as their additional Labour would be equal to that of 500 more"[36] (my italics). Here we have a clear assumption by an intelligent contemporary that it was not simply "the poor," the pauperized at the very bottom of the scale (though he makes them 23 percent of his total imaginary island population), who needed to be employed but also the agrarian populace who spent half their time idle.

Although the employment problems of the modern backward areas are obviously not identical with those of seventeenth-century economics, it is surely more than a mere coincidence that Law in 1705 should have assumed a state of affairs which has its remarkably close parallel in more than one under-developed economy today. There is nothing very new in all this. Ernle stressed the "scarcity of constant, and especially of winter, employment," which, he went on to say, "emphasizes the value to day labourers of commons and domestic handicrafts."[37]

This leads on to the related question: how far was domestic industry able to compensate for under-employment in agriculture? To some extent and in certain ways it must have been able to do so. The very ease with which an under-employed rural labour force (a "reserve army of labour" if ever there was one) could at once form the basis of a domestic cloth industry and at the same time contribute to increasing national agricultural output suggests that some measures of success must have been achieved in the course of time. Innumerable statements could be quoted, extolling the virtues of industry as an employer of the idle. Defoe went so far as to describe those regions where the only source of livelihood was agriculture as "unemployed counties."[38]

But it is equally clear that, as industry grew, this compensation became of less and less value. As is well known, the domestic industrial worker became increasingly dependent on industry and in many cases was an agriculturalist only nominally; consequently the pattern of his working life was shaped more by industry than by agriculture. Moreover, the irregularities of work inherent in the nature of domestic industry became more and more marked as the industry expanded. Nor was there any particular reason why these irregularities of work in one occupation should dovetail in with those of the other. On the contrary, it is highly probable that they often tended to coincide. Climatic conditions impeded both; the delays and irregularities in raw material supply in industry were often due to poor communications and primitive transport; the seasonal demand for agrarian labour at harvest time bore no organic relation to industrial demand. Moreover, the demand for industrial products was neither regular nor constant. Apart from the variations arising from poverty of communications along lengthening channels of demand, it is likely that much inconstancy of demand also arose from the variable and often unfavourable economic expectations of the age.

This source of under-employment was not confined to the "domestic" or "putting-out" methods of industrial production. These irregularities also bore upon the individual artificer and his servant, upon industries dependent on wind- or water-power and, perhaps to a lesser extent, upon those which used comparatively large capital equipment of one sort or another. In their study of medieval masons, Messrs. Knoop and Jones have shown clearly how the work of these craftsmen in the fifteenth century was subject to various discontinuities and how it was frequently casual, seasonal, or semi-permanent.[39] There seems little reason to suppose that circumstances were greatly different in the seventeenth century; similar conditions held for other building workers. To take a different example, the water-powered mill which, in one guise or another, was in such widespread use at the time, was frequently interrupted in its functioning, by drought in the summer, by ice in the winter, or floods in the spring. This was as true in other centuries as in the seventeenth; it applied to industries as diverse as paper-making or iron-smelting. All were harried by "the many Interruptions [which] they must receive from a Redundancy or Deficiency of Water, want of Materials, Intervention of Holy-days, and other Contingencies."[40]

The type of visible under-employment described so far was, from the labourers' point of view, involuntary. A further source of under-employment was that arising from the social habits of the community, i.e., voluntary under-employment and in particular a marked preference for leisure instead of higher earnings, the phenomenon known to economists as a backward-sloping supply curve for labour.

One form which this took was the frequent observance of sundry saints days, feasts, and the like, which almost certainly owed less to the demands of piety than to the attractions of the tavern. Holidays were irregular. The regular holiday goes with regular work: irregular holidays with irregular work. Many economic writers commented upon the preference for leisure instead of higher earnings. Thomas Manly, for instance, observed in 1669 that "the men have just so much the more to spend in tipple, and remain now poorer than when their wages were less. . . . They work so much the fewer days by how much the more they exact in wages."[41] Petty, Houghton, Law, Child, Cary, Pollexfen, and Roger North were amongst others who said, in one way or another, that when real wages were high, labour was voluntarily idle, that low corn prices meant high labour costs.[42] It was said of agricultural workers and of industrial, of urban as well as of rural.

This phenomenon is not simply a product of the labourer's life being, as Furniss put it, "caught fast in the clutch of custom and rigid tradition," of his wants being few, nor of his being "circumscribed . . . by the rigid policies of nationalism."[43] It is a normal part of the backward economy in which the volume and variety of cheap consumer goods is small, in which economic horizons are strictly limited both on the demand side and on the supply side. It is a reflection of the tight circle of physical and economic circumstances which contrive to keep the poor poor quite apart from the interventions of policy, at once by reacting on production as well as on consumption.

Irregularity of work of this type was not confined to the working week. The working day at one end of the scale, the working year at the other, were both very different from their counterparts in the modern industrialized community. The regularity, consistency, and intensity of work which the latter demands were quite alien to the worker of the seventeenth century and indeed of Tudor England.[44] The regularity of hours of work and of conditions of employment which the Statute of Artificers attempted to lay down in 1563 was a tribute to the non-existence of that regularity. Within a decade or so of its enactment there are complaints of non-observance:[45] hiring by the year, labouring constantly from morning to evening with regular breaks—such things did not happen. A hundred years later, the message is the same: "It is found by daily experience that several persons both men and maidens fit to go to service do . . . either lie at their own hand out of service or else put themselves to service for half a year or three-quarters of a year as they see good and then lie at their own hands again, whereby they get a habit of idleness, laziness and debauchery."[46]

A further item of complaint was "running and shifting from town to town and from country to country"[47] (i.e., county to county). Labour, as is more and more being understood, was far from immobile in these earlier centuries.[48] The relevant clauses of the Statute of Artificers, the Settlement laws and other measures designed to restrain mobility are, once again, more reasonably to be interpreted as a testimony to the existence rather than the absence of what they sought to prevent. A fair amount of labour mobility would seem a likely concomitant of involuntary under-employment. The drift townwards was a feature of the times as it is in many backward economies of today. Unskilled or semi-skilled migrants found their way into lowly paid jobs: servants, pedlars, and petty dealers, casual work of one sort or another. In Lichfield in 1695 nearly 11 percent of the entire population over the age of fourteen were domestic servants in households.

These, then, are the keynotes of a great deal of work at that time: irregular, under-employed, taking on the character of casual labour. Such conditions arise, in part at least, directly from the extreme limitation of man's control over natural forces. In industry particularly it stems from the absence of fixed capital equipment capable of operating independently of the immediate interference of nature.[49] Just as demographic conditions provided the basis for many of the problems of poverty, so did these conditions form the background of the desire to "employ the poor." It was the basis, too, not simply of the economists' desire to maintain or stimulate employment for the good of the national economy, but of the government's desire to do so for the sake of public order. Casual labour is a good basis for a mob, and a mob a valuable part of a well-organized riot.

V

The medium- or short-term elements or the forces not necessarily inherent in the nature of society are well known, and there is no need to elaborate upon them. Indeed, many of the developments or attitudes of the time have often been ascribed to these elements, to the exclusion of the long-term forces. The so-called price revolution, the eviction of peasants from their holdings, periodic trade depressions—to such particular phenomena as these are often attributed not merely the timing and especial nature of legislation, economic attitudes, or social behaviour, but much also that in reality rests on the basic framework of society. This is not to suggest that these elements were unimportant; it is to suggest, however, that they need to be fitted in with the enduring forces. There is the question, for instance, of how far rising prices meant falling real wages in this period. It is very probable that this aggravated the problems of poverty. Here it will suffice to stress that this trend reinforced the tension between policies and underlying forces in the economy. It at once added force to the upward pressure on wages and provided a further justification for, as well as influencing the timing of, the Statute of Artificers as a major codification of wage policy.

Three developments may be selected for some brief attention in order to illustrate their relation to the long-term forces. They are the changing attitude towards the question of the size of population, the sharpening of international competition in the textile industry, and the increase both in frequency and severity of fluctuations in economic activity.

As mentioned earlier (see above, p. 112), it was in the second half of the seventeenth century that the desire for a large or larger population was put forward emphatically and frequently. In the later decades of the sixteenth century and at the beginning of the seventeenth century, a number of writers were concerned with the possible dangers of too many people. What lies behind this change?

Some of the difference is more apparent than real, for it rests upon the relative absence of a body of economic theorizing in the sixteenth century and its corresponding growth in the later seventeenth century; that there is ample evidence of firmly held views in one period does not necessarily mean that such views were not held earlier. Indeed, there is evidence that they were. The contention, put forward in 1549, that the realm should be "thorrolie inhabited"[50] was a typical one; fewness of people was in no way approved; even such writers as Hakluyt and Malynes stressed the merits of large populations;[51] and, by the 1650s, Harrington was putting forward the desirability of stimulating population growth.[52] Much of the talk of overpopulation came, as is well known, from the enthusiasts for colonization, and special pleading doubtless had its part to play. The fact remains, however, that a number of writers seem to have been convinced between roughly the 1580s and 1640s that this country had, in some way, too many people and that emigration was to be encouraged.[53]

From the information at present available it is not possible to say whether these opinions were supported by any real demographic changes. But scattered and diverse evidence does point to the possibility that population was increasing at an appreciably faster rate in the sixteenth century than in the seventeenth. When Hakluyt asserted in 1584 that "throughe oure longe peace and seldome sickness wee are growen more populous than ever heretofore"[54] he (and others after him) may have been pointing to real influences of demographic importance. Conversely, the seventeenth century, ushered in by the famine of 1596–97, brought renewed and severe outbreaks of plague, more harvest failures, wars, worsening climatic conditions, and various other pointers towards higher mortality and a markedly reduced rate of population growth.[55] This is very largely hypothetical, and much work on English demographic history needs to be done before it can be otherwise.

Such a hypothesis then needs to be considered in relation to the attitude to employment. In both periods, the need for employment was stressed, but there is a difference in emphasis. In the earlier period, faced with the reality or the memory of the unemployed, the vagrants, the displaced persons of Tudor England, the emphasis is upon the danger to the State and the social order. Emigration, as in other countries and at other times, seemed a likely remedy for unemployment. But in the later period the writers were not confronted with the same manifestations. They were becoming increasingly aware of visible under-employment and at the same time they were anxious for an increasing exploitation of home resources, so they made the explicit link between the wish for more people and more employment. Increased food production and perhaps a decreased rate of population growth had removed the fears expressed earlier of pressure upon the means of subsistence; furthermore, the intensification of international economic competition had made more hands seem increasingly desirable, techniques being what they were.

This leads on to the second point mentioned above: the growing competition in the cloth industry. This generated a force bearing upon wages. The cloth industries in a number of continental countries were growing rapidly, especially from the later decades of the sixteenth century. France and Holland were amongst the countries where cloth manufacture was developed behind tariff walls designed to shut out English wares. The growth of foreign competition figures amongst the findings of the Commission of 1622; by 1632 it was reported that not only in Holland, but in such places as Brandenburg, Silesia, Poland, and Prussia, cloth was being produced which drove out the more expensive English product.[56] This trend of competition in manufactured goods continued throughout the century, accompanied by tariff wars. In a system in which labour is the outstanding factor of production and in which the substitution of capital for labour is severely limited because of the absence of technical knowledge, much of the weight of competition falls upon labour as a factor of production. Not wholly: some certainly found its outcome in the search for new markets and in diversification of products.[57] But insofar as it fell upon labour it had its effect in generating a further downward pressure on wages which, in turn, reinforced the tendency, also inherent in the "domestic system," towards poor workmanship, theft of raw materials, and the like. It is the pressure of such forces as these, in their interaction with the longer-term elements, which lies behind the clamour over the low wages in the cloth industry, the legislation at the turn of the sixteenth century attempting to enforce minimum wages in textiles, and the renewed efforts to regulate industry after the barrage of complaints in the early years of the seventeenth century about the "false and deceitful" wares made in England.

In precipitating these measures, or in intensifying the relevant discussions, it is the short-term elements which are vital. They need not necessarily be cyclical movements of the same type as those in the modern economic world. They may, and of course they did, owe much to crop failures or the visits of epidemic disease, to political crises or the ravages of warfare; or they may owe something to financial panics or to the inventory cycle which is part and parcel of the importance of trade. It was such as these which brought acute unemployment, a worsening of poverty and distress, sometimes starvation. But they did *not* bring the chronic under-employment any more than they alone brought irregularities of work. Hardship caused by trade depressions was not, of course, new to the seventeenth century, but its frequency and intensity may well have grown during that century, along with economic expansion, growing competition, and the increasingly violent interruptions of the warfare of the time.

To take simply the question of warfare. Aside from the ill-effects of war itself, the growth both in size and in frequency of use, in seventeenth-century England, of both army and navy almost certainly aggravated the discontinuities of working life. Impressment into the fighting forces was a peculiarly appropriate method of recruitment in a society where labour already knew little consistency of work or regularity of employment. Recurrent warfare, conducted on an increasingly large scale especially in the second half of the century, was not conducive to steady economic growth or to the increased constancy of employment which contemporary writers so much wanted to see. The rapid and spectacular growth of the navy, for instance, saw it become "in some respects the largest industry in the country,"[58] and certainly one peculiarly liable to fluctuations in employment. The sharp fluctuations, for example, simply in the growing numbers of those who worked at the dockyards,[59] lead one to ask what happened to those workers when they were periodically laid off from the yards. Whence were they recruited? What was the pattern of their working lives? How far did such dockyard work add a further element of the casual to what was already irregular?

VI

To return, in conclusion, to the questions asked earlier in this article. The attitudes, both of writers and of the government, towards labour were rooted in the position of labour in the economy of the time. They cannot be explained simply in terms of the continuity of particular types of policy, nor as a part of a system of nationalism. Similarly, it is impossible to explain them simply in terms of individual attitudes or the actions of particular writers or statesmen. This is not to suggest, however, that they are explicable solely in terms of social and economic forces. There is no point in enthroning a mass of impersonal forces, even for the sake of bringing about the abdication of that impersonal monarch "mercantilism."

The position of the labourer was not a prison from which none could escape, any more than was the attitude to labour some fixed object incapable of being shifted, within a certain range of reasonable limits, by contemporaries with a gift for action or analyzed and modified by those of originality. But as a first step to examining economic attitudes, it seems not unreasonable to ask economic questions about economic forces. This certainly implies some belief in a positive relationship between forces and ideas; and it may also imply some exercise in economic model-building. Both are anathema to those who sniff determinism on every breeze. But without the use of such tools of inquiry, the social and economic analysis of communities in the past, their functioning and their ideas, cannot adequately proceed. The ultimate alternative is social and economic antiquarianism. Policy may have its continuity, nationalism its vigour and individuals the last answer in shaping events. But for the sort of inquiry we are concerned with here, we must look beyond them to examine not only economic forces but also the tensions which come into being between those forces and between the forces and the attempts to regulate and control them. These forces and tensions are neither anonymous nor sterile. They are made manifest in attitudes and in ideas; they evince themselves, be it in cowed resignation or eruptive violence, be it amongst rural labourers or urban merchants.

The study of policy itself can be most misleading; it can usually shed only an indirect light upon the true nature of the economy. The sheer weight and number of regulations, the very fact of which is a part of the impact of a highly developed state power upon an under-developed economy, have too often led us wrongly to equate their existence with their observance. Nor is the power or the effect of such decrees to be equated with the power or effect of forces operating within the economy. One of the first things we need to do if we want to learn more about the English economy of the seventeenth century, and within it the position of labour, is to start by jettisoning that misleading and cumbersome portmanteau, that unnecessary piece of historical baggage—the idea of "mercantilism."

CHAPTER 3

1. Based on a paper read to the Annual Conference of the Economic History Society, April 1955.

2. "Every one but an idiot knows that the lower classes must be kept poor or they will never be industrious," Arthur Young, *Farmer's Tour through the East of England* (1771), iv, 361.

3. *E.g.*, "The surest Wealth consists in a Multitude of laborious Poor," quoted E. Heckscher, *Mercantilism* (1934), II, 164.

4. Peter Chamberlen, *The Poor Man's Advocate* (1649), p. 30.

5. C. Davenant, "An Essay upon the probable methods of making people gainers in the balance of Trade," in *Works,* ed. Sir Charles Whitworth (1771), II, 184–5.

6. J. Pollexfen, *A Discourse of Trade, Coyn and Paper Credit* (1697), p. 41.

7. Thomas Fuller, *The Worthies of England* (1662), ed. J. Freeman (1952), pp. 202–3. On this whole question of employment, see E. Furniss, *The Position of the Labourer in a System of Nationalism* (New York, 1920), and Heckscher, *op. cit.,* II, 145–62.

8. J. Cary, *An Essay on the State of England in Relation to its Trade, its Poor and its Taxes* (Bristol, 1695), pp. 143–50; Sir Dudley North, *Considerations upon the East India Trade* (1701), quoted in T. E. Gregory, "The Economics of Employment in England, 1660–1713," in *Economica* I, (1921), 45–60.

9. Sir Josiah Child, *A New Discourse of Trade* (1693), p. 95.

10. *Brittania Languens* (1680), in *Early English Tracts on Commerce,* ed. J. McCulloch (repr. 1952), p. 349.

11. *Op. cit.,* II, 167.

12. Heckscher, *op. cit.,* I, 19.

13. *Ibid.,* II, 167.

14. W. D. Grampp, "Liberal Elements in English Mercantilism," *Quart. J. Econ.* LXVI (1952), 468.

15. There is some discussion on these lines, tucked away in Appendices in Furniss's work, mixed up with the details of industrial policy and the Poor Law in E. Lipson, *The Economic History of England* (1947) (4th ed.), III, chs. V and VI, or involved in Heckscher's study with his ingenious, but not entirely convincing, argument about protectionism and "the fear of goods."

16. This approach envisages something very similar to that outlined in W. W. Rostow, *British Economy of the Nineteenth Century* (Oxford, 1948), ch. VI, though with rather less emphasis on cyclical and purely economic phenomena.

17. Quoted Lipson, *op. cit.*, III, 484.

18. Gregory King, *Natural and Political Observations* (1696), reprinted in G. Chalmers, *An Estimate of the Comparative Strength of Great Britain* (1820), pp. 424–5.

19. D. V. Glass, "Gregory King and the Population of England and Wales at the end of the Seventeenth Century," *Eugenics Rev.*, XXXVII (Jan. 1946), and "Gregory King's Estimates of the Population of England and Wales, 1695," *Population Stud.*, III (March 1950).

20. W. G. Hoskins, "An Elizabethan Provincial Town: Leicester," *Studies in Social History*, ed. J. H. Plumb (1955), p. 45. See also W. G. Hoskins, *Industry, Trade and People in Exeter, 1688–1800* (Manchester, 1935); D.C. Coleman, *The Economy of Kent under the Later Stuarts* (unpublished Ph.D. Thesis, London, 1951); and J. Thirsk, in *Victoria County History, Leicester*, II, 227–8.

21. See, in general, Lipson, *op. cit.*, III, ch. VI, and Furniss, *op. cit., passim*.

22. M. D. George, *England in Transition* (Penguin ed., 1953), p. 10.

23. R. Baxter, *The Poor Husbandman's Advocate to Rich Racking Landlords*, ed. F. J. Powicke (1926).

24. Figures in (i) from D. V. Glass, *op. cit.* in *Population Stud.*, III, and H. Gille, "The Demographic History of the North European Countries in the Eighteenth Century," in *Population Stud.*, III, (June 1949); those in (ii) and (iii) from *The Determinants and Consequences of Population Trends* (United Nations, 1953), p. 143, and calculated from figures in *U. N. Demographic Year-Book* (1953).

25. Comparison of Sweden in 1750 and the U.S.A. in 1952 appears to cast doubt on this general proposition; there is reason to suppose, however, that Sweden's under-15 percentage was lower than average (cf. its slow rate of population growth) and the U.S.A. similarly stands apart, for obvious reasons, from the main European trends. The figures given in K. J. Beloch, *Bevölkerungsgeschichte Italiens* (Berlin, 1937), I, 23–58, for the age-structure of various Italian states in the same era offer further confirmation of the general position. The 0–15 percentage in the town and province of Sorrento in 1561 was 34 percent, of Capri in 1591, 41 percent, of Conselve in 1737, 38 percent; for males only, the relevant proportions in Vicenza in 1585 and for Belluno and Cadore in 1640 were respectively 42 percent, 37 percent, and 33 percent.

26. See L. I. Dublin, A. J. Lotka, and M. Spiegelman, *Length of Life* (New York, 1949), ch. II.

27. Cf. *Processes and Problems of Industrialization in Under-Developed Countries* (United Nations, 1955), p. 17 n. where the identical figure of 67 percent is given as the proportion of the population in industrial countries today which fall within the "economically productive age bracket" of fifteen-sixty-five, as compared with 57 percent in under-developed countries.

28. See Glass, *op. cit., Population Stud.*, III. I am grateful to Professor Glass not only for lending me his typescript copy of this enumeration but also for giving generously of his advice on demographic matters.

29. The numbers over sixty were very probably exaggerated, though there is no reason to suppose that this significantly alters the relation between the pauper and non-pauper.

30. Cf. the figures in Beloch, *op. cit.*, which show some markedly lower figures for the towns than for whole provinces; the relevant proportions for Florence and Padua at dates between 1622 and 1663 ranged from 27 to 31 percent. In Sweden in 1757, when the percentage for the whole country was 34.5, that for Stockholm was 24.6; see Per Wargentin, *Tables of Mortality in Sweden* (1766) (Stockholm, 1930).

31. See Chalmers, *op. cit.*, pp. 433–4.

32. Quoted Lipson, *op. cit.*, II, 61. Later, Thomas Hardy put it in another way in *The Mayor of Casterbridge* (1895), p. 101, ". . . Your mother was a very good woman— I can mind her. She were rewarded by the Agricultural Society for having begot the greatest number of healthy Children without parish assistance, and other virtuous marvels.

"'Twas that that kept us so low upon ground—that great family. Ay, where the pigs be many the wash runs thin."

33. See Heckscher, *op. cit.*, II, 155–7.

34. Davenant, "Essay," *op. cit.*, p. 202.

35. The literature on under-employment is considerable but very scattered. The above examples were derived from R. H. Tawney, *Land and Labour in China* (1932), pp. 52–3, 120–1; *The Times*, 24 August and 14 September 1954; Chiang Hsieh, "Under-employment in Asia," *International Labour Review*, LXV (June 1952).

36. John Law, *Money and Trade* (Edinburgh, 1705), pp. 97–8.

37. Lord Ernle, *English Farming Past and Present* (1938), p. 300.

38. *Plan of English Commerce*, quoted Heckscher, *op. cit.*, II, 156.

39. D. Knoop and G. P. Jones, *The Medieval Mason* (Manchester, 1933), pp. 129–41.

40. Library of H. M. Customs and Excise: Excise-Treasury Letters, 1733–45, fol. 247. This comment was made by the Commissioners of Excise in regard to paper mills. There is ample evidence to show that it was true in practice. For an example in iron-making, see A. Raistrick, *Dynasty of Iron Founders* (1953), pp. 107–9.

41. Thomas Manly, *Usurie at Six Per Cent* (1669), quoted Furniss, *op. cit.*, p. 120.

42. See Furniss, *op. cit.*, pp. 119–25.

43. *Op. cit.*, pp. 234–5.

44. "Divers artificers and labourers . . . waste much part of the day . . . in late coming unto their work, early departing therefrom, long sitting at their breakfast, at their dinner and noon-meat, and long time of sleeping afternoon." Thus ran a complaint of 1495. (Quoted Knoop and Jones, *op. cit.*, p. 117.)

45. See *Tudor Economic Documents*, ed. R. H. Tawney and E. Power (1924), I, 360.

46. Kent County Archives, Maidstone: Quarter Sessions Records, Canterbury, 1682.

47. *Tudor Econ. Docs.*, I, 360.

48. See, *e.g.*, E. Buckatzsch, "The Constancy of Local Populations and Migration in England before 1800," *Population Stud.*, V (July 1951).

49. It is, in passing, interesting to note that a much larger flow of complaints about

idleness and the like seems to have come from England and France than from Holland; the limitations of man's achievements in industry were very much more striking than in trade and finance in which a high degree of ingenuity had been apparent at an early date.

50. "Policies to reduce this realme of England unto a prosperous wealthe and estate," in *Tudor Econ. Docs.*, III, 314.

51. E. A. J. Johnson, *American Economic Thought in the Seventeenth Century* (1932), pp. 49–54.

52. C. E. Strangeland, *Pre-Malthusian Doctrines of Population* (New York, 1904), pp. 116–17.

53. K. E. Knorr, *British Colonial Theories, 1570–1880* (Toronto, 1944), pp. 41–8.

54. Quoted Knorr, *op. cit.*, p. 42.

55. See, e.g. W. G. Hoskins, "The Rebuilding of Rural England, 1570–1640," *Past and Present*, (November 1953), pp. 53–7; E. G. Hobsbawm, "The General Crisis of the European Economy in the Seventeenth Century," *Past and Present*, (May 1954), pp. 34–5, and the authorities quoted therein; G. Utterström, "Climatic Fluctuations and Population Problems in Early Modern History," *Scand. Econ. Hist. Rev.*, III (1955).

56. H. Heaton, *The Yorkshire Woollen and Worsted Industries* (Oxford, 1920), pp. 190–3.

57. See F. J. Fisher, "London's Export Trade in the Early Seventeenth Century," *Econ. Hist. Rev.*, 2nd ser., III (1950).

58. J. Ehrman, *The Navy in the War of William III, 1689–97* (Cambridge, 1953), p. 174.

59. See my article in *Econ. Hist. Rev.*, 2nd ser., VI (1953), 139–45.

If the small and divided, if expensive, bureaucracy of Early Stuart England failed to provide much of a prop for the Stuart monarchy, the growth of the electorate contributed positively to the increasing instability of seventeenth-century English politics. Further, if the pervasive patriarchalism encouraged the subject to adopt a stance of deference and obedience to his rulers, the growth of the electorate both increased the size of the political nation and encouraged its active participation in at least one aspect of the governing process. Christopher Hill's "many-headed monster" in a different guise became the enfranchised free-holders—virtuous, liberty-loving, and worthy of being cultivated by local worthies and party leaders alike. In this essay J. H. Plumb explains what is known about the causes of the growth of the electorate, about the nature of the choices facing the expanding political nation, and the degree to which those choices were real, and finally about the impact that growth had on the nature and structure of seventeenth- and early eighteenth-century English politics.

Dr. J. H. Plumb has been Professor of Modern English History at the University of Cambridge since 1966. He is the author of two political biographies: Chatham *(London, 1953) and the yet to be completed* Sir Robert Walpole, *of which two volumes (London, 1956, 1960) have so far appeared. Among his recent works are* The Growth of Political Stability in England, 1675–1725 *(London, 1967), an immensely suggestive study of the process by which a century of revolution came to an abrupt end, and a collection of essays,* In the Light of History *(London, 1972), which suggests something of the range of his historical interests and sympathies. The present essay first appeared in* Past and Present, *45 (1969), 90–116, and is here reprinted by permission of the author and of the Past and Present Society, Corpus Christi College, Oxford, which holds the world copyright.*

The Growth of the Electorate in England from 1600 to 1715*

J. H. Plumb

Representative governments have had a very chequered history during the last four hundred years of Western history: common in the late Middle Ages, they were mostly suppressed or ignored by the second half of the seventeenth century. Their relationship with monarchy and their rôle in national government have been more closely studied than their social bases. Furthermore, although the idiosyncratic development of England, where the representative assembly strengthened at a time when others had floundered or were floundering, has been noticed often enough, the reasons for that survival have not been satisfactorily explained. Not only did Parliament in England survive in the seventeenth century, but also it fathered a notable sub-species in those colonial assemblies which marked the representative institutions of America. And whatever we may think of seventeenth- and eighteenth-century Parliaments, the men of the enlightenment regarded them as bulwarks of liberty: a gleam of hope in a Europe dark with oppression.

For a generation the English contributions to social and political liberty have not engaged the attention of scholars, perhaps because such a preoccupation might seem to be tainted with whiggery and its misguided interpretation of English history. And the essentially English origins of American revolutionary ideology were also politely ignored, a situation now corrected by Professor Bernard Bailyn.[1] There is at last a clearer realization that the American

---

*This article is based on a paper given at the Conference of British Studies held at the University of Kansas in October 1968.

colonies shared a common political and social culture with Britain. They were parts of the same polity. Moreover, not only were the American institutions of government of the same family as those of Britain, but they suffered the same ills, the same genetic weaknesses. The intention both of Parliament and of the colonial assemblies was for a mixed government in which the competing forces in society were balanced: the representative assembly guarded liberty and insisted on economy, which they knew would be constantly threatened by the very nature of monarchical or gubernational government. Parliament preserved those liberties which the world envied all Englishmen. Yet by 1700 these had been constantly threatened for over a hundred years, indeed not only threatened but nearly extinguished by the Stuarts. And the Augustan Parliaments were suffering new and more insidious setbacks from a cunning and power-hungry executive that used places, contracts, honours, promotions, and bribes of every kind to undermine the nation's fundamental liberties. And in the early eighteenth century the suspicions which had been focused on the monarchy were being transferred to the ministry. And the same is true in the American colonies: the protection of American interests against exploitation by Britain was felt to depend not only on the burgesses in their assemblies, but also on the voters who sent them there. The ultimate bulwark of the nation's liberties, English or American, was those who exercised the franchise.

> You are called [wrote John Trenchard, appealing to the freeholders before the election of 1722] the Mobb, the Canaille, the stupid Herd, the Dregs and Beasts of the People and your interest is never thought of by those men who thus miscal you. . . . For my own Particular [he went on] I cannot give myself leave to despair of you, because I must at the same time despair of old English liberty: You are our Alpha and Omega, our first and last resource and when your virtue is gone, all is gone.[2]

And what political propaganda, written in England, was more popular in America than Cato's letters? The political base of both societies rested on the enfranchised freeholders. And it is this social base of Parliament that has been constantly ignored. Parliamentary relations with the monarchy and the executive were not its only relationships of importance. Parliament, in the seventeenth century, was a representative institution, and representative of a large and constantly growing body of men—the freeholders of England: a body which contemporaries never ignored.

By Trenchard's day the freeholder had, however, been exhorted for generations to avoid the wickedness of men intent on corrupting him and so destroying his true principles. In 1634, John Preston admonished electors and told them "it is an error among men to think that in the election of burgesses . . . [they] may pleasure their friends or themselves"[3]—implying that if the freeholder voted for godliness, the Commonwealth would be secure. From Preston to Trenchard, the freeholder had been the target of a deluge of pamphlets which urged him to follow his true principles.[4] But "true principles" ranged from a love of the Church and a loyalty to the monarchy to a passion for liberty and a horror of arbitrary power. What is clear, however, is that everyone assumed that there was a voter to be persuaded or cajoled.

By Walpole's day millions of words had been printed in electioneering pamphlets: they lie thick, dusty, and rarely disturbed on our library shelves.[5] Although nominally sold, they were usually given away in bulk by their sponsors to be distributed to taverns, coffee houses, and voters of local standing and importance.[6] Now if it is true that, as Namier said, not one in twenty voters exercised his franchise freely, but merely did the bidding of his landlord, or as Professor Walcott would have us believe for Queen Anne's reign, that county elections were more often than not settled by the nobility and gentry between themselves, this pamphleteering would seem to be a fatuous waste of time and a shocking waste of money.[7] Or was there, as these generations of pamphlets would imply, an electorate in 1700 to be persuaded; or a sufficient number of voters whose own private decision on whom to vote for could sway elections this way or that? And if there was such an electorate, when had it come into being, for the sixteenth century witnessed no such propaganda as this? And how had this electorate grown, steadily or by fits and starts? And, more important still, how extensive was it and how free? And, most important of all, what influence did it have on the nature and structure of English politics? It is to such questions as these that I am, with the help of other scholars, now addressing myself.[8] This essay is a first report, very tentative, and one that exposes problems rather than offers solutions.

About the early history of the electorate, whether of boroughs or of counties, we know next to nothing, a field of research which for the fifteenth and sixteenth centuries badly needs cultivating. We know, of course, that the qualification for the county voter was fixed at 40s. freehold in 1429, although the reasons for this and the social standing of those to whom it gave the vote are still somewhat obscure.[9] Certainly by the end of the sixteenth century the forty-shilling freeholder had acquired a semi-sacrosanct status, and I know of only one proposal at any time that the qualification should be either raised or lowered, except of course during the Civil War and Protectorate.[10] This qualification was seriously affected by the inflation of the sixteenth century. Initially this aroused, as far as I know, no comment. The reason for this could be that the electorate counted for very little before the 1580s when there are indications of an awareness of the freeholders' potential value. It was not until James I's reign that the gentry realized fully that the freeholder could be a source of power in their ideological disputes and personal feuds.

From the indications that we have, however, the Tudors do not seem to have liked a large electorate. In 1489, the Commons abolished the right of the citizens of Leicester and Northampton to vote in Parliamentary elections by Act of Parliament. Also, whenever one can catch an actual glimpse of elections in Star Chambers proceedings, there are strong indications of a similar attitude. When at Chichester in 1584, the candidate of the commoners told a leading member of the corporation that he must please the people, he was rebuked sharply. "No, no," Edward More told him, "the people must be governed, not pleased." Needless to say the commoners' candidate lost the election. These sentiments—fear of the voice of those not within the magic circle of the self-perpetuating oligarchies of the Parliamentary boroughs—find numerous echoes elsewhere. In Gloucester in 1584, the city magistrates told the Earl of Leicester "that experience hath taught us what a difficult thing it hath always been to deal in any matter where the multitude of burgesses have voice"[11]—a difficulty which most corporations took pains to avoid.

By the 1580s there are hints that the potential value of the voter was being realized and also that an increase in their number might help those who desired a more godly commonwealth. In 1587, in a moment of exasperation, John Field, the ardent Puritan, leader of the classis movement, burst out to a colleague, "Tush, Mr. Edmunds, hold your peace. Seeing we cannot compass these things by suit nor dispute, it is the multitude and people that must bring the discipline to pass which we desire."[12] As we know, the Puritans had been exceedingly active in the elections for the Parliaments of the 1580s, and this is the decade when we get the first hints of appeal to a wider franchise in order to defeat the entrenched corporation oligarchies. In one case, Warwick in 1586, a Puritan extremist, Job Throckmorton, forced his election by threatening to invoke the rights of the commonalty to vote.[13]

"Men of the meaner sort" did not in Tudor or Stuart England take themselves forty miles across a county in order to vote for a man they did not know or for men of whose principles they were ignorant. Neither did humble tradesmen challenge their masters in the Guildhall about who should represent them in Parliament unless provoked to do so. If these Tudor freeholders were becoming active, it was because they were becoming recognized as useful by men who wished to get into Parliament. The electorate, if not created, was at least conjured up. And for the sake of true godliness even the insecure would take risks and on the question of godliness even humble men might feel capable of judging their social superiors, especially when instructed from the pulpit by a man such as Cartwright, whose presence at Warwick antedated Throckmorton's bid for the election. Also there are hints that, in these elections, country gentlemen were beginning to marshal their freeholders: indeed so many Puritans were returned in the 1580s, overturning old loyalties and established connections, that it is difficult to understand how this was done without a more skillful exploitation of the electorate than had been customary.[14] Certainly the hints are sufficiently strong for a closer study of the Elizabethan electorate to be very much worth while.

When, however, we reach the reign of James I and the early Parliaments of his son, there is no question of hints, no question of scraps of evidence; the evidence about the electorate is clear and unequivocal. The floodgates were opened by the Commons victory in Goodwin's case in 1604, a well-known triumph but still underestimated in its importance for the development of Parliament and the seventeenth-century constitution. Hitherto, disputes about elections had tended to find their way to Star Chamber; but, owing to James I's foolishness, for he threw away a strong legal case, the Commons became their own masters, immediately deciding not only whether a person or a category of persons might sit in the House, but also the validity of elections.[15] The validity of the election might have been limited to contraventions of due processes, but the Commons took upon themselves the more fundamental questions of Parliamentary franchises, the revival of representation in boroughs where it had lapsed, and even the question of new enfranchisement, matters hitherto regarded as falling within the prerogatives of the Crown. Not many Parliaments were to pass before the Commons were laying down, in their resolutions, general principles about the nature of the franchise. Many attempts were made with varying success to secure a comprehensive bill to regulate election methods and in 1621 this bill contained clauses to alter the franchise. Some of these facts have been long known if insufficiently stressed, but what has been totally ignored is the consistency of the pressure by some members of the Commons on matters relating to the electorate, the exceptional vigour of this pressure from 1621 to 1628 and the connection between this pressure and a change of fundamental importance that was taking place in the electorate itself.[16] It was these years which saw Parliamentary representation secure a wide social base without which the Stuarts might have had far less difficulty in securing control of the corporations and so reducing the power of Parliament or abolishing it altogether.

There is an irony here that needs to be stressed and to which I will return later. It was the invasion of the gentry into the representation of the corporate boroughs that not only gave these towns larger electorates but also strengthened their constitutional rôle.[17] Had the usual legal requirements that resident burgesses be elected been rigorously maintained, the Commons would have been a far less formidable body. It was this victory, the snatching of borough representation by the gentry from nominees of courtiers and aristocratic families and from local merchants and patricians, that gave Parliament much of its strength to oppose the Crown. The struggle for political power was as intense in the electorate as in the Commons.

However, the more precise question of the growth of the electorate must be explored. In the counties inflation produced the voters; so there was no need to create them by other means. Indeed, it would seem that those members of the Commons who were most active in electoral matters, amongst whom Hakewell, Glanville, Henry Poole, and Sir George Moore were to the fore, were well aware both of the devaluation of the freeholder qualification and of the injustice of excluding the modest copyholders. In 1621 the bill to regulate elections contained a clause by which the freehold was to be raised to eighty shillings a year, but copyholders of ten pounds a year by inheritance added. This probably would not have diminished in any way the size of the electorate, but altered its composition. However, the large county electorates were more active than they had been. There were more contests and they were more hotly contested. The Commons made great attempts to secure fair and just elections. They severely rebuked the sheriffs of Cambridgeshire and Yorkshire who refused a poll when demanded, and even insisted that Thomas Wentworth should undergo another election.[18] Both sheriffs had publicly to acknowledge their fault at Quarter Sessions. Again the Commons resolved that the taking of names of freeholders at the poll was improper, as pressure might be subsequently applied on the freeholder because of his vote.[19] Of course, polls continued to be evaded and lists of freeholders composed, but these resolutions of the Commons express a political attitude. Another aspect of the same mood was the denunciation of letters of recommendation:[20] as Sir George Moore insisted, "Free Choice, so Free Voice." Such,[21] however, remained a hope and never became a reality in county elections. Personal influence continued to be rigorously asserted. And the gentry, of course, continued to organize their freeholders,[22] but with one, two, three, sometimes four thousand men present at an election there could be no certainty as to how a contest might go. For the next hundred years contests in the counties were frequent. When as few as twenty or thirty voters might sway the decision one way or the other, there was always the possibility that the most careful organization of disciplined and committed freeholders might fail. In such situations the influence of political attitudes, of commitment to political and religious ideology, became much stronger. Inflation had increased the number of county voters. The gentry organized them and brought them to the poll because the gentry were divided—sometimes on personal issues, sometimes on territorial issues, sometimes on religious and political issues, and sometimes on combinations of all three. They mustered loyal men, neighbourly men, like-minded men. The multitudes were conjured up, but once conjured up they created a factor of uncertainty and the final decision as to who should represent the county no longer remained entirely in the hands of the gentry. True, their influence was paramount. They selected the candidates, but the final choice between them could be made by a small body of freeholders. Knowing this it became even more important to convince freeholders on issues as well as personalities.

In the very vital period in the development of the electorate between 1614 and 1628, the increase in county electors and the greater numbers of freeholders involved was only one aspect of what was taking place. There were even more significant changes in the borough electorates—an aspect of Parliamentary history which has not been noticed, yet it is of profound significance for the survival and development of representative government in England.

There are two aspects of the growth of the borough electorate in this period: one widely known, the other ignored. The borough electorate had grown since the Reformation Parliaments by the simple process of reviving the representation of boroughs which had sent members to Parliament in the past, but whose representation had fallen into desuetude, more often than not through poverty, the borough being unable or unwilling to pay the members' wages. Other boroughs had representation granted to them by the Crown. Sir John Neale has analyzed this process and demonstrated convincingly that the Tudor gentry, particularly those at Court, were responsible for this growth and that they controlled the representation so granted. Now almost all of these boroughs, revived or enfranchised, were small towns, principally little seaports. Their electorates, in consequence, were very small too. The franchise was usually confined to the important burgesses. More often than not they were expected to elect without question the names sent to them by their patrons.[23] Even these electoral crumbs add to the total number of those involved in sending men to Parliament. However, after 1621, through a cunning interpretation of Goodwin's Case, decisions about enfranchisements or revivals were no longer a matter for the Crown, but for the Commons, and the attitude of the Commons towards the electorate may be judged from what they did. In all the revivals for which they were responsible between 1621 and 1628, the franchise, except in one instance—Weobley—was declared by the Commons to be in the inhabitants paying scot and lot or in the inhabitant householders. This gave to even small towns such as Great Marlow or decayed towns such as Milbourne Port an electorate of 200 or more. There is a remarkable consistency about the franchises of boroughs revived by the Commons: indeed this is also true of those re-enfranchised by the Crown. But it is a totally different principle. All but one of the Crown's—Evesham—were given an extremely restricted franchise. The towns revived by the Commons, it is true, were not selected because they were heavily populated. They were the result of a judicious combination of Hakewell's learning and the desire of the opposition to strengthen itself. Hakewell and his friends acted as ideologists often do, upon the principles in which they believed (that is that the franchise should be in the inhabitants), but also in their own self-interest (it was applied to small market towns where their influence was uppermost).[24] Nevertheless, wide franchises create large electorates, and no matter where they may be sited, large electorates require more care in management, more cajolery, more argument than tiny bodies of twenty or thirty. And the boroughs which the Commons revived had wide franchises and initially they were not easy to manage.

This brings us to the second aspect of electoral growth—that made by decisions of the Commons. Between 1621 and 1628, time and time again the Commons voted in favour of a wider franchise. There is no space here to go through case after case and a few examples must suffice. At Sandwich in 1621, the Commons overrode the Privy Council decision that the right to election was in the Mayor and Jurats and insisted that the commoners had a right to vote.[25] At Chippenham the electorate was widened and taken out of the hands of the thirteen capital burgesses.[26] At Pontefract, a revived borough, it was resolved that, as there was no charter, "the Election is to be made by Inhabitants, Householders, Resiants,"[27] a far wider franchise than freemen. In 1624, the Commons laid down a general principle, arising from their discussions on the contested election in Cirencester,

> there being no certain custom nor prescription who should be the electors and who not, we must have recourse to common right which, to this purpose, was held to be, that more than the freeholders only ought to have voices in the election; namely all men, inhabitants, householders, resiants within the borough[28]

—echoing the decision which they had taken in regard to Pontefract in 1623. Colchester, Boston, Oxford, Warwick are other examples of the Commons widening the electorate.[29] The process was continued in 1640.[30]

The leaders in this development were, of course, lawyers and members who were suspicious of the influence of the Crown and its servants. These decisions demonstrate quite clearly that they felt that an extension of the electorate was in their interest. Their arguments also hinted at natural right, although couched in historico-legal terms.

An even more interesting development, however, was taking place in many towns without the intervention of the Commons. The Elizabethan borough electorates were small and approached in remarkably oblique ways. It is true that already one or two towns had large open electorates,[31] but this type of constituency appears to be rare. Towns such as Lincoln, Exeter, Reading, Oxford, Cambridge, Leicester, Northampton, King's Lynn, and many others did not recognize the right of the freemen or inhabitants to vote. The normal process was for the mayor and aldermen to select candidates and for the Common-Council men to approve. There were variations of this process, but in almost all of these major boroughs, the effective electorate was confined to the closely knit, intimately related borough oligarchies which provided the aldermen and Common-Council men. During the early seventeenth century this method of election began to change: sometimes helped by a decision of the Commons, but often not. Exeter allowed the freemen a voice in 1627 and this was confirmed by the Commons.[32] We know far too little about this process, but the results were remarkable. Although for towns such as King's Lynn and Cambridge the electorate had only risen from 51 to 300 and 24 to 200 respectively, Lincoln, Northampton, Leicester, Exeter had acquired electorates of nearly a thousand, electorates which continued to grow in size during the rest of the century. This movement in the major cities from a closed to an open electorate is of vital importance, for it was a process that the Stuarts desperately attempted to reverse. The greatest stumbling block to Parliamentary management was always the counties and the great cities; and the great cities, by and large, acquired their large and open electorates in the early seventeenth century, probably many of them between 1614 and 1628.

Why did this happen? We do not know. No historian has hitherto remarked on this vital development in the growth of the Parliamentary electorate. It will need to be explored in depth. Had this development been confined to one or two boroughs one might have presumed that it was the result of purely local circumstances, but the widespread nature of the change and the comparatively short time in which this growth seems to have taken place would argue that it was the result of a political attitude that had become widespread; that there were men, bent on power, who felt that they were more likely to secure it if the basis of Parliamentary politics was widened. Who were they? As yet we do not know. We may surmise that those members of the Commons who took pains in election matters—Hakewell, Glanville, Henry Poole, Sir George Moore, and others associated with them—and who time and time again demanded far wider franchises, were also active outside the Commons. This group will need further study. Many were lawyers and they justified their attitude on grounds of ancient inherent right of freeborn Englishmen. This is clear from the debates in the Commons and their decisions. The situation in the boroughs is, however, obscure and so far I have gleaned but few indications. Most local historians have not noticed the change which took place.

However, there are bits of evidence which point in certain direc-
tions. At Exeter, the first signs of pressure from the freeholders
came in 1588 and 1593, when the Corporation conceded that the
Common Council had the right to alter their choice. However, the
Common Council accepted what was offered them. The issue was
forced by Ignatius Jourdain, who was Member of Parliament for
1621 and 1625, but not elected by the Corporation in 1626. He,
however, got himself elected in the open county court and he
repeated this performance in 1627, when the House of Commons
confirmed his election. This established the freemen's right to vote;
the franchise, however, was not extended to the freeholder until
1689.[33] Nevertheless, Jourdain's victory extended the franchise
dramatically. Ignatius Jourdain, the effective champion of the
franchise, was a Calvinist and a leader of the Puritans in Exeter.
Furthermore, Jourdain was supported by John Hakewell, sheriff of
Exeter and the brother of William Hakewell, M.P., one of the
leading lights of the committee which dealt with disputed elections.
He had been deeply involved in the abortive bill for franchise
reform in 1621, another to regulate elections, and of course in the
revival of the Buckinghamshire boroughs in 1624. Members of the
Exeter corporation had stayed with him in London when disputing
the Bishop of Exeter's claim to nominate a justice of the peace for
the city.[34] When further research is done, I think that we shall find
that the men active in opening the franchise were Puritans, often
lawyers, sometimes merchants, frequently country gentlemen. Certainly the freemen, and the freeholders and the inhabitants, must
have been aroused, organized, and led by some men of influence.
It is unlikely that citizens in King's Lynn or shopkeepers in Reading
assembled of their own accord to insist on a right to vote. But
whatever the reasons, the electorate grew fast between 1614 and
1628. But it did not stop then. The Commons in 1640 possessed a
vigorous champion of large electorates in Sir Simonds D'Ewes, who
believed as sincerely as any Leveller that the poorest man had a
right to vote unless charter or ancient custom denied him that
right. And in this view D'Ewes had the support of several members.[35] They were successful in widening several franchises. Not all,
however, much to D'Ewes's chagrin. To the despair of what he
called "the religious and sound men of the House," Salisbury was

lost and Edward Hyde and Michael Oldsworth seated on a narrow franchise: too many M.P.s being swayed, D'Ewes thought, by the fact that Oldsworth was secretary to the Earl of Pembroke.[36] Indeed, I doubt whether the majority of M.P.s were ever very sympathetic to a wider franchise. After all, the bill of 1621 failed to become law and the frequent bills to regulate elections never did any better than the bills to regulate drunkenness. Success came from an effective pressure group that was very strong indeed on the Committee for Privileges and Elections; and they exploited their superior knowledge (far, however, from accurate) of constitutional precedents and tried to establish general constitutional principles about the franchise. They had many successes, but they also had their failures. Nevertheless with each Parliamentary election in the reigns of the first two Stuarts, the electorate had grown considerably. By the Long Parliament it reached down not only to the minor gentry and rich merchants, but to yeomen, craftsmen, shopkeepers in the majority of towns and all the counties.

This enfranchisement took place for the sake of political power. The value of the elector and his vote increased with the growth of strong ideological differences in the gentry about religion, taxation, and the role of Parliament and the monarchy. To sway his mind, to persuade him to the hustings, to secure his vote by every art became a vital preoccupation with all who were concerned with government. Hence the first four decades of the seventeenth century witness the growth and burgeoning of strictly political propaganda written to influence voters and the development of broadsides and ballads for similar purposes.[37]

Also there are signs that men of "the meaner sort" were no longer at the disposal of their masters. Contested elections for county seats occurred occasionally in Elizabethan Parliaments, and from the Star Chamber proceedings to which they occasionally gave rise, Sir John Neale has described them to us in detail. They raised violent passions, but the passions were territorial or personal: bitter feuds between families or of different sides of the counties; occasionally, as in Rutland in 1601, a few sharp epithets about religion might be thrown out in the shouting and jostling and general hurly-burly of taking a view of the voters.[38] The personal element, however, was totally dominant. Certainly family conflict had not vanished in 1640 and the most recent historian of Kent maintains that family and clan issues decided the elections both to the Short and Long Parliaments in that county.[39] Indeed there is evidence to support this view, letters of Sir John Sedley to Sir Edward Dering telling of the machinations of neighbours or the promise of others to deliver their tenants. The correspondence between the principal gentry involved in the election scarcely mentions issues. And no one can doubt that clan and family, social and territorial standing, played their parts. There were few families in Kent in 1640 who could aspire to have a Knight of the Shire and their rivalry was acute. But does it really seem probable that a highly populous county, rich in small gentry as well as yeoman freeholders, would totally ignore issues in 1640? Within two years men would be killing each other for issues. As well as leading families, there were voters. Sir Edward Dering knew it. That he canvassed widely is well known. But now we have his personal reckoning of his voters and also his account of the election of 1640, material that has hitherto eluded the historian of this period.[40] Sir Edward Dering's list of freeholders is nearer akin to the lists drawn up by candidates in the Elizabethan period, prior to the day of election, so that they could be checked at the poll, than to a poll book of the late seventeenth century, although it possesses some resemblance to this. It is, however, the earliest embryonic poll book that we have, some thirty-eight years before the next. It lists those who promised themselves to Dering and those who voted for him; lists some who defaulted and some who voted for his rival, Sir Roger Twysden. It is a half-completed document and many parishes are blank: presumably Dering found the task too onerous for his own labour. Fortunately, however, he appended, largely it would seem to relieve his feelings, an account of the election and of the reasons which he thought caused his defeat. From the lists which Dering did draw up, it is clear that many who had promised did not finally vote for him: possibly thinking that the poll might last for days, they had gone home; possibly having heard discussions in the groups of freeholders and gentry at Penenden Heath, they changed their minds. Of some there is no doubt: of sixteen freeholders of Smarden, Dering noted "these of Smarden defaulted."[41] In many parishes it was obvious that promised votes did not materialize at the actual election. This hardly looks as if the gentry could deliver their freeholders *en bloc*. The reasons Dering gives for his failure, apart from the chicanery of what he called "the warping Sheriff," were that "The obscure[42] and puritanical that are separatists & lovers of separation did make itt theire cause to have a child of theires in ye House. no paynes was enough for them: and what they will, they will do pertinaciously."[43] That is the Puritans had been earnestly canvassing. Equally destructive were the rumours which Dering said were current about him. He listed them. They were these:

Entred in opposition to my Lo Chamberleyne.
Entred in opposition to Sr Hen: Vane.
Entred in opposition to ye Deputy Leiuten.
Was a commissioner for ye Knighting money.
Was ye cause that shipping money was payd.
Is another Buckingham.
Will not go to ye rayles att communion.
Is a papist.
Is a patentee for wine.
Called ministers hedge-preistes.
Can not endure Bishops.
Set up first altar in Dover Castle.
My wife keepes popish pictures.
Is a courtier.[44]

Although several of these are contradictory, no one could deny that the majority are ideological and that they touch the burning issues—religious and financial—of the previous eleven years of royal rule. In 1640 in Kent, issues were present; the personal position of candidates towards them discussed: and we know that freeholders or the minor gentry who led them could change their minds. This is undeniable. And Kent is no different from Suffolk, Essex, Norfolk or other counties where the evidence is also clear:[45] an electorate running into thousands could not be mustered like sheep or ignore the world in which it lived.

Dering calculated that 10,000 were present at Penenden Heath, an obvious exaggeration even allowing for hundreds of local sight-seers, hucksters, and the like, but well over 2,000 registered their votes. These were certainly present for a whole day, possibly longer, and it is unthinkable that such a concourse brought together for a political act should have avoided either a discussion of politics or the relationship of the leading personalities to them. Dering quickly recognized the facts of life and not only made his peace but forged an alliance with the Puritan group and at the election for the Long Parliament he succeeded in defeating Twysden's candidate. He discharged this debt by proposing the Root and Branch Bill although he did not stay long allied to the Parliamentary opposition. I would not suggest for one moment that the support of the Puritan element or its withdrawal was the most critical factor in this election.[46] It was one factor. The family connections and alliances of the Derings another. But family connections and alliances were now entangled in political issues that smouldered with political violence. The extent of the electorate, partially swayable by these issues, as well as by loyalty towards or fear of their betters, had become a factor too in county politics. In 1640 the situation in the counties as well as the boroughs had changed out of all recognition from Elizabethan times, and we witness the birth of a political nation, small, partially controlled, but no longer co-extensive with the will of the gentry. It could not be called by the most fervent stretch of the imagination democratic, and yet the political system was no longer purely oligarchical. Nor did very many of the gentry view this extension of political interest and activity with a great deal of favour. Their attitude probably chimed with Lord Maynard's, who vowed after the Essex election of 1640 never to appear again at "popular assemblies whear fellowes without shirts challeng as good a voice as myselfe."[47] Indeed the gentry of Essex had every reason to fear the yeomen and weavers of Essex, for they had driven the Catholic Lady Rivers helter-skelter out of the county, seized Sir John Lucas, the Royalist, before he could quit his house. Their revolutionary zeal, not altogether unwelcome to the House of Commons, had scared the local Parliamentarians out of their wits.[48] As in Essex, so in Suffolk and a dozen other counties. The rumblings of the lower classes, bitterly anti-Catholic and anti-Royalist, or rather anti-Establishment, were too loud for their ears. And yet to survive, as Mrs. Pearl has shown in her excellent study of London, the Parliamentary forces could not entirely rely on the sympathetic tycoons. They were forced to a wider base—to citizens and apprentices.[49] And once forced to it, they had to indoctrinate, to educate their supporters in politics and in religion. Nor were they alone in discovering either this necessity or its value. The Levellers were soon preaching, exhorting, talking of the rights of the Commons of England, and discussing an electorate so extensive that it made both Cromwell and Ireton wince with horror.[50]

The Civil War was one long, troubled, baffling, political education. And the Commonwealth was but the second act. It should be remembered that between 1653 and 1660 there were more Parliamentary elections than there had been for the previous thirty years. The old nexus of families and interests, if not entirely destroyed, were fractured and broken, enabling new men and their allies to taste the sweetness of social status and political power, and even to weave in some boroughs and some counties a new pattern of obligation and so consolidate a basis of loyalty, founded on common political attitudes that had not only powers of survival, but also of growth. The political upheavals of the Commonwealth in counties and in Parliamentary boroughs have scarcely been studied, yet it is here, I suspect, at the very grass roots of political power, that the struggles began that were to lead to the great conflict between Whig and Tory for the rest of the century.[51] Also what is so often forgotten in the study of Cromwell is that he attempted to find an equitable and broad base for government amongst the propertied classes. Quite contrary to his own political security, he increased to the point of absolute dominance the Knights of the Shire and abolished the little oligarchical boroughs with their tiny electorates. Kept firmly in the hands of the propertied classes, nevertheless within these limits the Cromwellian franchise was quite fairly distributed, even though the franchise was less, far less, generously interpreted than before the Civil War. Cromwell's franchise was fixed at a high level—the possession of £200 in real or personal property. It was less than he and Ireton had seemed willing to concede when at Putney the Levellers had pressed for an almost universal male suffrage (only conceding the exclusion of servants, apprentices and beggars). By 1648 the question of the electorate had become a burning issue, central to the debates about fundamental rights and questions of sovereignty. When the Level-

lers demanded a vote for all inhabitants, this arose from their experience of county elections, from what they had seen and heard,
not from abstract theory. They were carrying to a logical conclusion the policy introduced by the Puritan leaders in the House of
Commons between 1614 and 1628. A great deal of debate from
1640 to 1660 revolved about the proper base for political power,
the proper rôle, that is, for the electorate.[52] The electors were a
fact of political life: the county elections with their thousands of
voters created more than an air of representation and participation. The gentry had to convince and cajole as well as exert their
social authority or browbeat their poorer neighbours. Those who
fought for Parliament were deeply conscious of the problem of the
decayed boroughs and the influence this might create for men of
great property and they were eager to rationalize the borough
system and make their franchises akin to the counties. However, the
point which I wish to stress here is that the fact of the emerging
electorate, both in the boroughs and in the counties, helped to
create the issue of representation and the debates about it. The
Levellers, as well as Ireton and Cromwell, drew their ideas from
their experience of the facts of political life, particularly elections
to the House of Commons.

The issue of the electorate and of the franchise was central to the
Restoration settlement. Indeed the prospect of that settlement was
certainly eased by the reversion to the old franchise which took
place in 1659. The Convention Parliament showed its sympathies
for a wide franchise by declaring for it in all disputed elections, in
which the evidence allowed them the opportunity of doing so, a
policy which was immediately reversed by the Parliament which
met in 1661.[53] Charles II, and more particularly James II, knew
where the danger lay. They longed, both of them, for a more
autocratic and settled form of government. They remained deeply
suspicious of Parliament. And neither of them succeeded in man-
aging one for long. They tried out all methods. They had some
success, for they never met a Parliament, not even between 1679
and 1681, in which they did not have powerful and numerous
allies. Throughout the century the majority of the propertied
classes were deeply suspicious of political and constitutional crisis
for fear that it would encourage "the multitude." Nevertheless, to

balance the power of the monarchy, some felt that they had to lean towards it. Shaftesbury, who was no democrat, could only hope to overcome the loathing of the King for Exclusion by rousing the mass of the electorate by playing on their twin fears of popery and arbitrary government.

The Exclusion Parliament knew where their safety lay—in the mass of freeholders who turned up to the elections in such numbers that the Tory candidates gave up the contest on sight. Whenever there was the slightest chance, the Exclusion Parliaments declared for the widest franchise in the Parliamentary boroughs. They knew well enough that beyond the leading gentry families, beyond even the lesser gentry and pseudo-gentry, there were yeomen, husbandmen, craftsmen of every kind—bakers, weavers, stocking-frame knitters, butchers, men of small substance —for whom political and religious issues were no longer a matter for their betters. Their political education had not stopped with the Restoration. Pamphlets, newsletters, ballads, the growth of coffee houses and clubs, the development of cross-posts and better stage-coaches allowed ideas to travel fast. There was growing up in England a politically conscious nation, not coterminous with the population, but far wider than the large-property-owning classes, far wider even than those who exercised the franchise, great though this was becoming.[54]

After the Revolution of 1688, the situation changed dramatically. General elections became very common indeed, averaging in Queen Anne's reign about one every two and a half years. Contested elections in every type of borough became commonplace. Some constituencies were contested far more frequently than their equivalents in the nineteenth century. As we know, party passion ran high, and the struggle between Whig and Tory became a bitter one. To control electorates became a matter of vital importance. The methods by which this was achieved and their effect on politics I have described elsewhere. One development which I noticed in *The Growth of Political Stability* was the printing of poll books.[55] The poll book served a variety of purposes. One was that it was sometimes difficult to challenge freeholders willing to swear to their freehold at the poll, whereas once their names and villages were in a candidate's possession, he could study them at leisure and use what he discovered to challenge the result at the Bar of the House of Commons if he could afford to do so. More importantly these books demonstrated to the organizers of both parties where their strengths and weaknesses lay; where more canvassing might be needed for future electoral contests. They also showed whether promises had been kept or broken. Indeed by Queen Anne's reign they had come to be regarded as almost essential for every constituency with a large electorate. We know of the existence of 101 poll books for Queen Anne's reign alone and there are probably many, many more to be discovered, for, unless they were printed, which was usual only for the counties and not always even for them, they tend to survive in a single copy. Although they have been known, they have never been systematically used: indeed they have scarcely been glanced at. But through them we can investigate the nature of the electorate in detail, get through to the actual voters and discover how they cast their votes in election after election.

The size of the electorate is astonishing. In 1640, Suffolk had an electorate of approximately 3,000, very large by the standards of the time; by 1710 this electorate had grown to 5,500 or more—in fact the electorate had nearly doubled, and perhaps some 500 voters were added in Queen Anne's reign.[56] Such a growth is typical of the electorate as a whole. From preliminary calculations the electorate rose, at a conservative estimate, from 200,000 in William III's reign to 250,000 by the end of Queen Anne's. It may indeed have been much larger than this, for reasons which I will return to later. However, a quarter of a million voters, using Gregory King's figures for the total population, gives a percentage of 4.7 who possessed the vote, whereas after the Reform Bill only 4.2 percent did so. In 1832 the spread of the electorate was, of course, somewhat more equitable, but that is another considera- tion. As a percentage of adult male population, of course, the figure would be far higher: probably about 15 percent or above. Obviously it is extremely important to know who constituted this electorate. One would like to know how literate it was, how much it was under the control of the landlords and gentry. Was it, as it were, born to its political commitment, voting Whig or Tory election after election, or can one discern commitment to leading families and figures that overrule other considerations? How deep into the population did the electorate penetrate? Many of these questions cannot be answered yet and we shall be many years before we can give solid, statistical answers, for the amount of material is huge and no work of any sort has, to my knowledge, been done on it. It will need many hands and many hours of computer time to make this material yield all of the information that is buried within it. And, of course, the evidence is uneven—for Suffolk, for example, we have a splendid series of poll books for 1701, 1702, 1705, and 1710, whereas for Devonshire or Berkshire there are none. Again, in the boroughs, we have an excellent series for burgage boroughs, particularly Cockermouth, where there is a poll book for every election.[57] The owners of burgages wished to make sure that their dependents had cast votes as promised and also they needed the poll books to decide on possible points of attack, for at this time burgages in most boroughs were in many hands. Other types of borough, however, vary. Most large boroughs such as Norwich or Nottingham fortunately have one or two poll books.[58] Norwich poll books have the added interest that they give the occupation of the voters, so that we know, for example, that the overwhelming majority of the Norwich weavers were consistently Whig in politics, but that the butchers stayed Tory. The material, scattered as it is and sparse as it is for some regions and for some types of boroughs is, I am sure, sufficiently rich to yield an insight in depth into the political life of the nation such as no other source can give. These poll books will also, quite probably, throw considerable light, too, on the structure of the population as a whole, for, so far, the demographers have ignored these poll books as a source for the reconstruction of parish life, yet they list a large section of the middle and lower middle classes.

However, certain features of the electorate emerge from quite a cursory study of a sequence of poll books. Let us glance for a moment at Suffolk.[59] One is immediately struck by the number of voters who vote in one election only. This is true of the small villages as well as the market towns of the area. Let us take the tiny village, little more than a hamlet, of Westhorpe in the heart of Suffolk. In the four elections for which we have a record, eighteen freeholders voted, but ten of them in one election only. Only two freeholders voted in all four elections, one of whom was the richest man in the village, William Boyse, Esq. One man voted in three elections and five in two. Boyse's votes are interesting. In 1701 he voted Tory, in 1702 he voted Whig, Whig again in 1705, and back to Tory in 1710. Here indeed was a floating voter. I suspect Boyse was a patriot who rallied to the Whigs and the war and grew in the end disgruntled with both. The other regular voter was Thomas Rodwell. He was an immovable Tory, voting for the two Tackers in 1705. He was, of course, the village parson. Of the one who voted in three elections and the five who voted in two, all but one remained true to their allegiance and cast their votes for the same party. It is also interesting that most of the single voters occur in the 1705 election when the question of the Tack was a burning issue. Twelve freeholders, seven Whigs, and five Tories left Westhorpe for Ipswich in 1705, whereas only four voted in 1701, eight in 1702, and six in 1710. However, this high proportion of single voters is common elsewhere: it is quite clear that it is a phenomenon of the electorate of this time. What, as yet, one cannot be sure about is that the Tack brought these Westhorpe men to make the journey to Ipswich. It could have been the result of intensive canvassing at this election. It is just feasible that their presence is the effect of high social mobility. We may discover these freeholders at other elections, living in different Suffolk villages. Personally I think this very unlikely. I believe it was issues and canvassing that got the voters out then, as it does now. Other evidence would seem to support this view. Single election voters are extremely common in all villages and towns and may provide as much as 20 percent of the electorate at any given election which would give an almost lunatic rate of social mobility. Single election voters is one strange and important fact to emerge. But these books provide other evidence that is equally interesting. It is exceptionally rare to discover any village where the same voters go to election after election voting for the same party *en bloc*. Most villages were divided on party lines. I would estimate that over 90 percent of villages in Suffolk were divided in politics. Even in areas dominated by great landowners such as Sir Robert Davers, the high Tory Knight of the Shire, villages still have their Whigs. Thomas How and George Cocksedge in Daver's own village of Rougham insisted on voting against him. Of course the leading gentry could deliver a large number of votes from their tenantry, through loyalty, common interest, and, at times, fear, but there still remained a great number of voters who could not be dragooned, who insisted on going their own way. In almost every village there were committed party men, Whig and Tory: their reasons for being so will have to wait until we know far more about them.[60]

If we turn from the villages to the towns we find a similar picture. A large number of townsmen in Suffolk possessed a county vote and again we find the pattern of a small committed core on both sides, Whig and Tory, who vote in election after election and a large number of freeholders who turn up for one election only. In the three elections of 1702, 1705, and 1710 for Suffolk, ninety-one freeholders of Eye voted. Forty-six voted in only one election. This may be slightly too high, for there could be freeholders who voted in 1701 whom I have listed as one-timers for 1702; so the figures for 1705, eleven out of fifty-one voters, and 1710, seventeen out of forty-five, are more reliable, but even this confirms what we have noticed before: that there were many freeholders who were stirred to vote once but not again. And the reasons for this will need investigation, but it hardly looks like landlords driving their tenants to the poll. Of the more regular voters at Eye, there were five Tories who voted three times, ten Whigs who voted three times for their party, and two Whigs who voted Whig in 1702 and 1705, but who changed their party in 1710. Of those who voted twice, twelve were Tories, seventeen were Whigs, but again two of the latter deserted to the Tories, one in 1705, the other in 1710. From this it would seem that Whigs were more active. The single voters were split pretty evenly between Whigs and Tories—about ten in each election—so the slight margin which the Whigs maintained at Eye was due to the coherent and regular voting of the committed Whigs. There are signs, too, that a few Whigs grew disillusioned with the war and what drift there was in 1710 was from Whig to Tory. In the counties and large boroughs, a cursory inspection of the poll books indicates a considerable division on party lines, important floating voters, and less landlord control than has been suggested. The importance of the poll books diminishes somewhat as one moves from the counties and the great boroughs to the small corrupt boroughs of the South-West, but they still convey important and difficult facts. We get the same indication of growth and not contraction—that comes later, after 1715. Small boroughs, such as Cockermouth, Pontefract, and Weymouth all more than doubled their electorates and most of the Cornish seaports added voters during the late seventeenth century. What, however, is more interesting is that often these small electorates were not, as one might expect, very constant in their make-up: for example, at Mitchell in Cornwall, forty voted in the election of 1705, thirty-six in 1713, but there were only eighteen voters common to both elections. This may, of course, be explainable by specific circumstances at Mitchell, although it is difficult to see what they were.[61] The most surprising factor to emerge from our preliminary investigation of the electorate between 1689 and 1715 is for me this large turnover of voters in counties and boroughs, great or small. In boroughs as small as Mitchell, we may be able to solve this peculiar problem fairly quickly and the solution may throw insight on the larger problem of the counties.

From the poll books so far investigated it is clear that every constituency of any size had committed party men who voted in elections with the same regularity as many M.P.s did for their party at Westminster. They were life-time Whigs or life-time Tories. These were the most active and effective part of the constituency, turning out election after election. It is also clear, however, that some voters lost their faith and changed sides. There was a floating vote that could swing a constituency from Whig to Tory.[62] What is surprisingly rare in Suffolk, considering the size of the electorate, are voters splitting their votes, giving one to a Tory and the other to a Whig, as one might expect if clan or family issues were dominant. Single voters, plumpers, are rare too, at least in Suffolk.

It would, however, be quite wrong to think of this electorate as being totally free: quasi-feudal relationships still counted, men acknowledged their social leaders and followed them, bribery and threats were far from unknown. All the arts of persuasion and cajolery were centuries old by 1700. The evidence for that is voluminous, well known and incontrovertible. How effective it was needs to be tested by the evidence of the poll books. The fact remains that, as ministers, party leaders, and the gentry well knew, there was an electorate to be managed and one for which issues and political ideas carried weight. And it was by this electorate that the liberties of Englishmen were protected and secured, for they decided who should represent them, for this was the period when constituencies, great and small, frequently found themselves at the hustings.

As I have shown elsewhere, the very fact of a large electorate and the frequency of contests subtly influenced the nature of politics in the period.[63] The aim of the Whig leaders when married to the Hanoverian succession was to evade it, diminish it, or control it.[64] The gradual strangling of the electorate by the executive did not pass unnoticed. There was a powerful feeling that the fundamental liberties of Englishmen had been betrayed and that the foundations of parliamentary government had become worm-eaten: a situation that had many echoes with the political situation in the American colonies, so that *Cato's Letters* had the same ring of truth in New York or Norfolk. The freeholder had become in seventeenth-century England a political animal. No country in Western Europe had experimented so deeply as England with a qualified democracy, and when men talked of the liberties of Englishmen it was not idle rhetoric. It meant that tens of thousands of them, a very significant proportion of the male population, had the right to choose their governors after 1688: opportunities were frequently available for them to exercise that right in contested election after contested election. By the middle of the eighteenth century much of that birthright had been lost, hence both the bitterness of the *Craftsman* and the growth of a movement for reform.

We historians have been, perhaps, too concerned with the politics at the centre, with methods of manipulation and influence, and ignored the politics at the grass roots in the constituencies, where between 1688 and 1715 the voice of the electorate was able to make itself heard in many places. And it is now being realized, too, that this experience, in all its complexity, influenced the politics of America profoundly. I hope that before very long we shall know far more about this electorate: there is much to learn and we have a key, even though a most complicated one, in the poll books. One of the odder results may be to show that England was far more democratic between 1688 and 1715 than immediately after 1832, and much more dominated by party issues.

CHAPTER 4

1. See Bernard Bailyn, *The Ideological Origins of the American Revolution* (Cambridge, Mass., 1967); also his *The Origins of American Politics* (New York, 1968), and J. R. Pole, *Political Representation in England and the Origins of the American Republic* (London, 1966).

2. [Thomas Gordon and John Trenchard], *Cato's Letters,* 3rd edn. (London, 1733), iii, p. 11. For Trenchard, see Caroline Robbins, *The Eighteenth-Century Commonwealthman* (Harvard, 1959), pp. 115–25.

3. Quoted by Michael Walzer, *The Revolution of the Saints* (London, 1966), p. 259.

4. The growth of the political pamphlet in the first half of the seventeenth century and its proliferation in the second still awaits its historian.

5. Nineteen pamphlets were printed in February 1715, all directed at the freeholder's vote in the imminent general election: *The Monthly Catalogue 1714–17,* repr. by the English Bibliographical Society, 1st ser. (1964), pp. 57–63.

6. It was not always pamphlets that were distributed. In 1721, with an eye on the 1722 election, the earl of Sunderland had C. King's *The British Merchant or Commerce Preserv'd,* 3 vols. sent to every parliamentary borough for the use of the inhabitants: Godfrey Davies, *Bibliography of British History, Stuart Period, 1603–1714* (Oxford, 1928), p. 186. The past was also readily invoked. In preparation for the Yorkshire election in 1734, the Tories published, suitably edited, Sir John Reresby's *Memoirs* to justify Tory policy since the reign of Charles II; not to be outdone the Whigs published *The Revolution in Politics,* in serial form, eight cheap parts so that the poorer freeholders could afford to buy them: *Memoirs of Sir John Reresby,* ed. A. Browning (Glasgow, 1936), p. x, n. 1; J. H. Plumb, *Sir Robert Walpole* (1960), ii, p. 314.

7. L. B. Namier, *The Structure of Politics on the Accession of George III,* 2nd. edn. (London, 1957), p. 73; R. R. Walcott, *English Politics in the Early Eighteenth Century* (Oxford, 1956), pp. 9–10.

8. Principally Dr. W. A. Speck of Newcastle University, but the subject is huge and the pastures as plentiful as they are lush.

9. E. F. Jacob, *The Fifteenth Century 1399–1485* (Oxford, 1961), p. 415. Also M. McKisack, *Parliamentary Representation of English Boroughs during the Middle Ages* (Oxford, 1932); J. S. Roskell, *The Commons in Parliament in 1442* (Manchester,

1954). There is also a very valuable short article by K. N. Houghton, "A Document Concerning the Parliamentary Election at Shrewsbury in 1478," *Trans. of the Shropshire Arch. Soc.,* lvii (1961–4), pp. 162–5, where it is argued that there was a growing recognition "by the end of the fifteenth century that the electors might be faced with a choice of candidates, to be determined by a majority decision." However, this appears in a number of the cases cited to be a widening *within the corporation,* not an extension to voters outside it. For example, two corporations quoted by Mr. Houghton—Exeter and King's Lynn—were in fact closed and narrow electorates throughout the sixteenth century. The freemen in Exeter had no vote until 1627 (see pp. 150–1). King's Lynn did drop an elaborate procedure in 1525, when the twelve leading burgesses gave up the right to elect, but that right remained limited to the two corporate bodies—the twenty-four and twenty-seven. The freemen (about two hundred) did not secure the right to vote until the Long Parliament. *Hist. MSS Comm., 11th Report,* iii, pp. ix–x, 179. However, the extension, even if small and mainly within the corporate body, is worth more detailed study.

10. In the Parliament of 1621: see Wallace Notestein, Francis Helen Relf, Hartley Simpson, *Commons Debates 1621* (New Haven, 1935), pp. iv, 421–2 and below.

11. J. E. Neale, *The Elizabethan House of Commons* (London, 1949), pp. 261–72, 275.

12. Patrick Collinson, "John Field and Elizabethan Puritanism," in *Essays Presented to Sir John Neale,* ed. S. T. Bindoff, J. Hurstfield, and C. H. Williams (London, 1961), p. 159. Michael Walzer, *op. cit.,* p. 135, points out that these early Puritan divines, Cartwright, Rogers, Field, etc., were sons of skilled craftsmen or yeomen, typical forty-shillings freeholders in fact.

13. Neale, *The Elizabethan House of Commons,* pp. 250–4.

14. Collinson, *op. cit.,* pp. 153–5.

15. For example, irregularities at Shrewsbury were dealt with in April 1604: the following resolution was passed on 25 June 1604 "that from, and after the end of this present Parliament, no Mayor of any City, Burrough or Town corporate should be elected, returned or allowed to sit as a Member of this House." *House of Commons Journal* (hereafter cited as *HCJ.*), ii, p. 201; p. 296. For Goodwin's Case, see J. P. Kenyon, *The Stuart Constitution* (Cambridge, 1966), pp. 25, 27.

16. The only recent work of value on this subject is by Richard L. Bushman, "English Franchise Reform in the Seventeenth Century," *Jl. of British Studies,* iii (1963), pp. 36–56. However, the appendix to this article is inadequate.

17. Not all corporations succumbed to the gentry or even shared their representation with them. Of the members who represented Exeter between 1537 and 1640 only eight were from gentry families and these were elected in the sixteenth century: Wallace T. MacCaffrey, *Exeter, 1540–1640* (Harv. Univ. Press, 1958), pp. 224–5.

18. *HCJ.,* ii, pp. 556, 570–1, 677–8, 687, 801–4. For the Bill of 1621, see Notestein, Simpson, Relf, *Commons Debates 1621,* iv, pp. 421–2.

19. *HCJ.,* ii, p. 884. The Committee of Privileges "held it inconvenient to have them set down their names: because notice might be taken of them, to their prejudice."

20. Notestein, Relf, Simpson, *Commons Debates 1621,* iii, p. 412; iv, p. 446.

21. *HCJ.*, ii, pp. 158–60, 509. This attitude had a long history: see Neale, *The Elizabethan House of Commons.*

22. *HCJ.*, ii, p. 161: Bucks. Co. 1604. The sheriff "desired every gentleman to deal with his freeholder," which indicates clearly enough the relationship between gentry and freeholders; and this was always to be true of the majority, but see pp. 152–6.

23. Neale, *The Elizabethan House of Commons*, pp. 140–5. Over 50 percent of the boroughs in 1689 with electorates of less than five hundred votes, that is the most manageable part of the Commons, were the results of Tudor revival or enfranchisement, *i.e.*, the rotten part of the Constitution was a Tudor creation.

24. For the revival of Parliamentary boroughs, see the very valuable article by Lady Evangeline de Villiers, "Parliamentary Boroughs Restored by the House of Commons 1621–41," *Eng. Hist. Rev.*, lxvii (1952), pp. 175–202. Lady de Villiers, however, does not discuss the question of franchise. James I, who thought that there were far too many decayed boroughs sending representatives and refused to consent to the enfranchisement of Durham until Old Sarum was disenfranchised, nevertheless revived or created a few boroughs. They were:

1604 Evesham; Harwich
1605 Bewdley
1610 Tewkesbury
1614 Bury St. Edmunds
1615 Tiverton

Lady de Villiers points out that, apart from Bewdley, these were all towns of economic and social importance and she thinks the boroughs restored by the Commons compare very unfavourably with them. The Commons boroughs, she considers, were "rotten" from the start (*ibid.*, p. 183). However, in this she is mistaken. The franchise tells a different story. Harwich had thirty-two electors; Bewdley (until 1679) thirteen; Tewkesbury (until 1640) probably twenty-four; Bury St. Edmunds thirty-seven and Tiverton twenty-five—very convenient elections to control. I am uncertain about Evesham, where the franchise may have been in the freemen from its revival in 1604 which, if this is so, would have given it an electorate of around 250, about the same as Hertford. The boroughs revived by the Commons, however, had wide franchises, comparatively large electorates and were strongly contested. In these contests, the inhabitants played their part—unusual activities in a "rotten" borough. See M. R. Frear, "The Election at Great Marlow in 1640," *Jl. of Modern History*, xiv (1942), pp. 433–48. In 1640, the inhabitants of Great Marlow wanted to be represented by two opposition members whom they could trust, namely Peregrine Hoby and Bulstrode Whitelocke. As their leader, Toucher Carter, "a country fellow in plain and mean habit," told Whitelocke, "it being no corporation, all the inhabitants had their votes in the election, and most of the ordinary people would be for Hoby and Whitelocke" (*ibid.*, p. 438). So perhaps the boroughs revived by the Commons were not so rotten as they seemed. They certainly proved less manageable than James I's revivals. Once a wide franchise has been created and there are more than a hundred voters, the problems of patronage become more difficult, particularly in times of political crisis.

25. *HCJ.*, ii, p. 568.

26. *Ibid.*, p. 686.

27. *Ibid.*, p. 714.

28. *Ibid.*, p. 792; also John Glanville, *Reports* (London, 1775), pp. 107–8.

29. *HCJ.*

30. See J. H. Plumb, *Growth of Political Stability* (London, 1967), pp. 48–9.

31. Shrewsbury was probably the largest at about 450. Attempts, however, were made to enlarge this further in 1604 when the sheriff tried to poll the inhabitants: *HCJ.*, ii, p. 201.

32. MacCaffrey, *Exeter 1540–1640*, pp. 223–4. For other boroughs, particularly Reading, see E. C. Whitworth, "The Parliamentary Franchise in the English Boroughs during the Stuart Period" (London Univ. M.A. Thesis, 1920). For Hakewell's part in the revival of the Buckinhamshire boroughs, see Lady de Villiers, "Parliamentary Boroughs Restored by the House of Commons," pp. 175–90. Hakewell possessed an estate in Buckinghamshire.

33. MacCaffrey, *Exeter, 1540–1640*, pp. 199, 223, 273; J. J. Alexander, "Exeter Members of Parliament," pt. iii, *Report and Trans. of the Devonshire Assoc.*, lxi (1929), pp. 195–6; Frances Rose-Troup, "An Exeter Worthy and His Biographer," *ibid.*, xxxiv (1897), p. 252.

34. MacCaffrey, *op. cit.*, p. 218; Ferdinando Nicolls, *The Life and Death of Ignatius Jurdain* (London, 1654). Jourdain had experienced conversion as an adolescent whilst living in Guernsey. He had been "new borne."

35. D'Ewes's views were based on what he regarded as constitutional legality. He argued strongly on behalf of the right of the poor of Great Marlow to vote. "I moved that the poorest man ought to have a voice that it was the birthright of the subjects of England and that all had voices in the Election of Knights etc.": *The Journal of Simon D'Ewes*, ed. Wallace Notestein (New Haven, Yale Univ. Press, 1923), p. 43. On the other hand, he disapproved very much of the fact that the Commons in 1640 had accepted as valid many writs signed by the commonalty and not by the mayor or bailiff, who for D'Ewes were the only legal returning officers. For D'Ewes, as I suspect for most, it was not a question of extending the electorate, but declaring ancient rights. D'Ewes was a precisian, not a politician.

36. *The Journal of Simon D'Ewes*, ed. Notestein, pp. 431–2; D. Brunton and D. H. Penington, *Members of the Long Parliament* (London, 1954), p. 136 for Oldsworth; also Violet A. Rowe, "The Influence of the Earl of Pembroke in Parliamentary Elections, 1625–1640," *Eng. Hist. Rev.*, l (1935), pp. 242–56. Naturally the opposition did not wish to upset so powerful an ally as Pembroke: political necessity was stronger than their dedication to principles relating to the franchise. Yet there were others, apart from D'Ewes, who put them first. They were a minority.

37. It is remarkable that there is, as yet, no general study on the growth of the political propaganda in England. By the time Thomason's collection starts in 1640, it is fully fledged, but its origins are obscure. Its growth must be related to an awareness of opinion and a desire to influence it: that is, an electorate to sway. On this subject see Godfrey Davies, "English Political Sermons," *Huntington Lib. Quart.*, iii (1939), pp. 1–22. And, of course, there was just as much awareness by Charles I and Archbishop Laud of the need for propaganda.

38. Neale, *The Elizabethan House of Commons*, p. 135.

39. Alan Everitt, *The Community of Kent and the Great Rebellion* (Leicester, 1966), pp. 76–83.

40. Frank W. Jessup, *Sir Roger Twysden, 1597–1672* (London, 1965), p. 141, n. 1, refers to the existence of this MS. which had been bought by Sir Thomas Phillips (Phillips MS. 16083) in 1858. It was sold in the Phillips sale in 1967 and found its way, via a Kentish bookseller, to the Bodleian Library, where it is now: MS. Top. Kent e.6. The detailed lists deserve analysis.

41. It should be noted that Dering did not blame a landlord or one of the gentry for this default.

42. By "obscure" Sir Edward meant, of course, men of obscure birth, of low social standing.

43. Bodl., MS. Top. Kent e.6.

44. *Ibid.*

45. For these counties see C. A. Holmes, "The Eastern Association" (Cambridge Univ. Ph.D. Thesis, 1969), pp. 42–53.

46. Jessup brings out clearly the tangle of family and political issues that were involved in these elections: *op. cit.*, pp. 137–44.

47. Brit. Mus., Egerton MS. 2646, fo. 142. I am indebted to my colleague, Dr. C. A. Holmes, for this reference.

48. See Holmes, *op. cit.*, pp. 70; 82–4.

49. Valerie Pearl, *London and the Outbreak of the Puritan Revolution* (Oxford, 1966).

50. A.S.P. Woodhouse, *Puritanism and Liberty* (London, 1938), pp. 52–85.

51. Vernon F. Snow, "Parliamentary Re-apportionment Proposals in the Puritan Revolution," *Eng. Hist. Rev.*, lxxiv (1959), pp. 409–92.

52. Of course, the nature of the franchise was only one aspect of elections which troubled the opposition, whether it was the Parliamentary Puritans of the 1620s or the Levellers of the 1640s; they were concerned about the freedom of elections. The Levellers, unlike the Parliamentary opposition of the 1620s, were also concerned with the distribution of seats. There is no indication that this greatly troubled members in the 1620s; indeed the reverse is true. In their bill for 1621, they accepted that there would be boroughs with less than twenty-four voters: Notestein, Simpson, and Relf, *Commons Debates 1621*, iv, pp. 421–2.

53. Plumb, *The Growth of Political Stability*, pp. 40–1.

54. *Ibid.*, pp. 41–5.

55. *Ibid.*, p. 43, n. 1.

56. These figures are based on the Suffolk poll books for the general elections of 1701, 1702, 1705, 1710: in the possession of the West Suffolk Rec. Off. (1701, 1702 [Cullum Library]), the East Suffolk Rec. Off. (1710) and the Society of Genealogists (1705). I am indebted to Dr. W.A. Speck for the loan of his copy of the latter.

57. Cockermouth Caster, Leconfield MSS.

58. *The Poll Books for Nottingham and Nottinghamshire, 1710*, ed. Myrtle J. Read and Violet W. Walker (Thoroton Soc. Rec. Ser., 1957), p. xviii. The biographical index by Miss Walker is the only fully detailed analysis of a poll book that we possess as yet. Norwich poll books for 1710 and 1715 are in the Guildhall Library, London.

59. All the following details are taken from the poll books listed above.

60. The smaller the number of voters in a village, the more likely they are to vote Whig or Tory as a bloc. It is very rare for a village of more than six or seven voters to be unanimous in its politics.

61. The franchise at Mitchell was in the inhabitants paying scot and lot.

62. See also the valuable computer analysis of Hampshire by W. A. Speck and W. A. Gray to be published in the *Bull. of the Inst. of Hist. Res.* I am grateful to the authors for allowing me to see this.

63. *The Growth of Political Stability*, esp. chap. iii.

64. See my chapter "Political Man," *Man Versus Society in Eighteenth Century Britain*, ed. James L. Clifford (Cambridge, 1968).

Bibliographical Note

The standard bibliography for Stuart England is *The Bibliography of British History. Stuart Period, 1603–1714,* ed. Godfrey Davies; 2nd edition ed. Mary F. Keeler (Oxford, 1970), which is reasonably complete to 1961 or 1962. A shorter but more up-to-date guide has been compiled by William Sachse, *Restoration England, 1660–1689* (Cambridge, 1971) in the Bibliographical Handbook series published for the Conference on British Studies. David Berkowitz's forthcoming *The Seventeenth Century* is in the same series. In addition there are the relevant sections of G. R. Elton, *Modern Historians on British History 1485–1945: A Critical Bibliography 1945–1969* (London, 1970), which, as the title indicates, surveys the major work published between 1945 and 1969. The Royal Historical Society, and more recently the Institute of Historical Research, has undertaken the Writings on British History series: *Writings on British History 1901–1933,* Vol. III, *The Tudor and Stuart Periods 1485–1714* (London, 1968) is continued in eight volumes in the same series, compiled by A. T. Milne, which cover publications from 1934 to 1945; *Writings on British History 1946–48,* compiled by D. J. Munro (London, 1973), is the latest in the series. *Bibliography of Historical Works issued in the United Kingdom, 1966–70,* compiled by William Kellaway (London, 1972), is the latest in a useful series that now covers British publications since 1947.

In recent years the quantity of publication has made the bibliographer's task formidable indeed, and the student who wishes to discover the current state of scholarship in his field faces difficulties of equal magnitude. Besides reviews of books the *American Historical Review* publishes both lists of "Other Books Received" but not reviewed and the quite comprehensive "Recently Published Articles." The Historical Association publishes the useful *Annual Bulletin of Historical Literature;* the most recent volume, No. 56 (London, 1972), ed. by J. L. Kirby, covers publications for the year 1970. Articles on seventeenth-century England and in most cases reviews as well occur with some frequency in *Agricultural History Review, Bulletin of the Institute of Historical Research, Church History, Economic History Review, English Historical Review, Historical Journal, History, Journal of British Studies, Journal of Ecclesiastical History, Journal of the History of Ideas, Journal of Interdisciplinary History, Past and Present,* and *Recusant History.* For a comprehensive guide, see J. L.

Kirby, *A Guide to Historical Periodicals in the English Language* (The Historical Association, London, 1970).

Some recent surveys of the century in order of publication are J. P. Kenyon, *The Stuarts: a Study in English Kingship* (London, 1958), Christopher Hill, *The Century of Revolution, 1603–1714* (Edinburgh, 1961), and G. E. Aylmer, *The Struggle for the Constitution, 1603–1689: England in the Seventeenth Century* (London, 1963). J. P. Kenyon, *The Stuart Constitution, 1603–1688* (Cambridge, 1966) provides a very useful collection of political and constitutional documents and commentary. There is now a companion volume to Tawney and Power's older *Tudor Economic Documents* in Joan Thirsk and J. P. Cooper, eds., *Seventeenth Century Economic Documents* (Oxford, 1972). Several recent volumes offer collections of essays which attempt to grapple in a sophisticated way with a number of periods of seventeenth-century English history: Geoffrey Holmes, ed., *Britain after the Glorious Revolution, 1689–1714* (London, 1968); G. E. Aylmer, ed., *The Interregnum* (London, 1972); Conrad Russell, ed., *The Origins of the English Civil War*, and A. G. R. Smith, ed., *The Reign of James VI and I* (London, 1973). There are also several important collections of essays by authors whose work has done much to shape the way early modern Britain is presently conceived: Christopher Hill, *Puritanism and Revolution* (London, 1958), J. H. Hexter, *Reappraisals in History* (Northwestern University Press, 1961), and H. R. Trevor-Roper, *Religion, the Reformation, and Social Change* (London, 1967). Other recent collections which have articles of interest on seventeenth-century England are W. A. Aiken and B. D. Henning, eds., *Conflict in Stuart England* (London, 1960), H. E. Bell and R. L. Ollard, eds., *Historical Essays 1600–1750* (London, 1963), C. H. Carter, ed., *From the Renaissance to the Counter-Reformation* (New York, 1965), and H. S. Reinmuth, Jr., ed., *Early Stuart Studies* (Minneapolis, 1970).

Given the focus of the present collection of essays, social structure, and economic change merit special attention. There are now three surveys of the pre-industrial economy of England—Charles Wilson, *England's Apprenticeship 1603–1763* (London, 1965), Christopher Hill, *Reformation to Industrial Revolution* (London, 1967), and L. A. Clarkson, *The Pre-Industrial Economy of England, 1500–1750* (London, 1971)—the last of which has an excellent, up-to-date bibliography. A number of Charles Wilson's essays on the seventeenth-century economy have been collected in his *Economic History and the Historian* (London, 1969); several of W. G. Hoskins's articles have been reprinted in his *Provincial England* (London, 1965). Three other important collections are F. J. Fisher, ed., *Essays in the Social and Economic History of Tudor and Stuart England* (Cambridge, 1961), E. M. Carus-Wilson, ed., *Essays in Economic History*, 3 vols. (London, 1954, 1962), and W. E. Minchinton, ed., *The Growth of English Overseas Trade in the Seventeenth and Eighteenth Centuries* (London, 1969). Developments in the rural economy have been treated in Joan Thirsk, ed., *The Agrarian History of England and Wales*, IV, *1500–1640* (Cambridge, 1967), and Eric Kerridge, *The Agrarian Revolution* (London, 1967). Some important works on aspects of trade are B. E. Supple, *Commercial Crisis and Change in England, 1600–1642* (Cambridge, 1959), P. J. Bowden, *The Wool Trade in Tudor and Stuart England* (London, 1962), Ralph Davis, *The Rise of English Shipping Industry in the Seventeenth and Eighteenth Centuries* (London, 1962), and his brief but very useful survey *English Overseas Trade 1500–1700* (London, 1973).

For the relationship between demographic and social change, see Peter Laslett, *The World We Have Lost* (2nd ed., London, 1971), and J. D. Chambers, *Population, Economy, and Society in Pre-Industrial England* (Oxford, 1972), both of which have useful current bibliographies; developments in this rapidly growing field can best be followed in the journals *Population Studies* and *Local Population Studies*. A number of recent studies explore one or another aspect of social structure and change: Lawrence Stone, *The Crisis of the Aristocracy, 1558–1641* (Oxford, 1965), J. T. Cliffe, *The Yorkshire Gentry: From the Reformation to the Civil War* (London, 1969), A. M. Everitt, *Change in the Provinces: The Seventeenth Century* (Leicester, 1969), W. K. Jordan, *Philanthropy in England, 1480–1660* (London, 1959), Christopher Hill, *Society and Puritanism in Pre-Revolutionary England* (London, 1964).

For the reader who wishes to pursue further the question of the role of bureaucracy in seventeenth-century England, the place to turn is to G. E. Aylmer's *The King's Servants: the Civil Service of Charles I, 1625–1642* (London, 1961), and *The State's Servants* (London, 1973). Some of the issues raised by Plumb's article on the electorate can be explored further in J. H. Plumb, *The Growth of Political Stability in England, 1675–1725* (London, 1967) and W. A. Speck, *Tory and Whig: The Struggle in the Constituencies, 1701–1715* (London, 1970). Political attitudes and assumptions, and the forces shaping them, are treated diversely by M. A. Judson, *The Crisis of the Constitution* (New Brunswick, N.J., 1949), W. A. Greenleaf, *Order, Empiricism and Politics: Two Traditions of English Political Thought, 1500–1700* (Oxford, 1964), Michael Walzer, *The Revolution of the Saints: A Study in the Origins of Radical Politics* (Cambridge, Mass., 1965), David Little, *Religion, Order, and Law* (New York, 1969), C. B. Macpherson, *The Political Theory of Possessive Individualism: Hobbes to Locke* (Oxford, 1962), J. A. W. Gunn, *Politics and the Public Interest in the Seventeenth Century* (London, 1969), William M. Lamont, *Godly Rule: Politics and Religion, 1603–1660* (London, 1968), Christopher Hill, *The World Turned Upside Down: Radical Ideas during the English Revolution* (London, 1972), and the early chapters of Caroline Robbins, *The Eighteenth Century Commonwealthman* (Cambridge, Mass., 1959). A seminal study which attempts to grapple with the nature of cultural change in early modern England is Keith Thomas, *Religion and the Decline of Magic* (London, 1971). Politics itself and religion—the two subjects to which seventeenth-century Englishmen would doubtless have given pride of place—are here omitted, not, obviously, because they are unimportant, but rather because the essays in the present collection do not deal with either subject directly.

Index